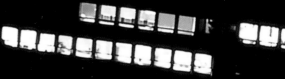

To Zoe
With love

Mum
x
Christmas 2006.

In the Headlines

The Story of the Belfast Europa Hotel

First published in 2003 by
Appletree Press Ltd
14 Howard Street South
Belfast
BT7 1AP

Tel: + 44 (0) 28 9024 3074
Fax: + 44 (0) 28 9024 6756
E-mail: reception@appletree.ie
Web-site: www.appletree.ie

A catalogue record for this book is available from the British Library.

In the Headlines - The Story of the Belfast Europa Hotel

ISBN: 0 86281 906 7

Editors: Jean Brown and Jim Black
Design: Stuart Wilkinson
Production: Paul McAvoy

9 8 7 6 5 4 3 2 1

In the Headlines

The Story of the Belfast Europa Hotel

Clive Scoular

Appletree Press

For all the dedicated and loyal staff of the Europa over the years

Contents

Foreword

By Senator George J. Mitchell

From 1995 to 1999 I was involved in the search for peace in Northern Ireland. The accord reached in 1998 has become known as the Belfast Agreement or the Good Friday Agreement. When it was reached I described it as an historic step. I also said that by itself it does not provide or guarantee peace and stability, but it does make them possible. Implementation of the Agreement remains the best hope for peace for the people of Northern Ireland. Much has been achieved; much remains to be done.

When in Northern Ireland I stayed at the Europa Hotel becoming, in the words of one of their staff, 'a semi-permanent resident'.

It is fitting that the Europa became the base for much of my work during this time. The fortunes of the hotel are a barometer for the wider situation in Northern Ireland. It has emerged from difficult times to outstanding success and provides a beacon of hope for the future. The renaissance of the hotel was epitomised by the visit of President and Mrs Clinton in 1995. I know their visit to Ireland will always have a special place in their hearts. The hotel's loyal and committed staff, arguably the most dedicated in the world, have given stalwart service through the good times and the bad.

During my stay in the Europa I became friends with many people in Northern Ireland and was overwhelmed by the generosity of spirit that staff in the Europa showed to me as the peace process developed. I will never forget the warmth and friendship of my 'landlord', Dr Billy Hastings, during this time. His foresight and effort turned one of the most bombed hotels in Europe into an outstanding business success. Billy and his staff who looked after me – John Toner, Carolyn Stalker, Martin Mulholland to name but a few – demonstrated the true spirit of Irish hospitality. I am grateful to them for making me welcome in Belfast.

The Europa Hotel in Belfast was a long way from my work as Majority Leader of the United States Senate. But it became a second home for me. I am an American and always will be. But Northern Ireland will forever have an important place in my heart. I have fond memories of the people of Belfast and the Europa. I congratulate them on their success to date and wish them the best for the future.

George J. Mitchell
Maine, 2003

Introduction

By the Chairman of Hastings Hotels Group
Dr William G. Hastings C.B.E.

I have always been an enthusiast for life and have never distinguished between work and pleasure. I enjoy them both equally and I have found that the energy and commitment expended on one aspect rubs off on the other. By approaching life in this way has meant that I have been enormously happy in both business and family affairs.

I inherited my work interests over forty years ago in the licensed trade which then grew to embrace wholesale, brewing and catering businesses. I went on to make hotel and property acquisitions which have flourished into the hotel chain of which I am now chairman.

Having always been fascinated by every aspect of the service industries, it gave me great pleasure to see the development in this sector grow so vibrantly. However nothing has pleased me more than to see the evolution of the hotel industry especially in Northern Ireland, given that its growth has mirrored expansion throughout the United Kingdom and Ireland and further afield.

But the emergence of the Europa itself, given all its trials and tribulations in Northern Ireland over the years, has helped to focus attention on the immense contribution which the hotel industry has made to every country's economy, particularly in regions otherwise bereft of income from other sources. It may be an imperfect theory but I consider that each and every city can be judged by the standard and quality of its hotels.

The city of Belfast has, in my opinion, greatly changed for the better since the arrival of the Europa Hotel and the many other fine hotels which have more recently set up in the city. The existence of these hotels greatly enhances the cultural life of any city. I have always been sceptical about doom and gloom statistics which have sent out conflicting reports about a city's so-called health. The best litmus test is to link first-rate hotel provision with entertainment available for their guests. Belfast nowadays exudes confidence and provides as high a level of both accommodation and culture as can be found anywhere on the island of Ireland.

The changes in the Europa, since it was opened in 1971, have precisely reflected what has been happening in Northern Ireland over those years. Conceived in the days of optimism in the 1960s, the hotel suffered through the traumatic years of the Troubles from the 1970s until the 1990s. Yet it has miraculously survived through the strength and resilience of its staff and its owners and stands today as a perfect testimony to its perfect pedigree.

From having the dubious reputation as the most bombed hotel in Europe over three decades, the Europa emerged as the hotel chosen by President Bill Clinton and his entire Presidential party in 1995. The words of the President, in a letter to staff in 2002, expressed clearly how much

Ireland would always have a special place in his heart and he also commended them on their strength of character over thirty difficult years.

This book tells the story of the Europa – from its evolution, its arrival on the scene on the Belfast landscape and its impact on the social fabric of the city. It tells of the good times and the bad times but, above all, it is a story of survival against the odds and represents a vision for the future of a vibrant and exciting city. It is the story of a nation reborn through the eyes of the Europa Hotel.

Railways and Hotels – Tourism springs to Life

Crowds line the streets of Belfast city centre. It is late on a dreary November afternoon in 1995. The light is fast fading. As the people anticipate the arrival of their visitor, they turn around and see the best known hotel edifice in the whole of Belfast, if not in Northern Ireland – the Hastings Europa Hotel.

Their trance-like state is suddenly broken as a screaming motorcade swings round the corner of Howard Street into the normally bustling thoroughfare of Great Victoria Street – Belfast's Golden Mile. The unwieldy bullet-proof stretch limousine comes to a halt outside the hotel. Trench-coated bodyguards jump out of the car and into the precincts of the hotel. Two people emerge, a man and a woman. The special visitors everyone has been waiting to see have arrived. They crane their necks to catch a glimpse as the couple turn and wave. A President of the United States of America is in town. After acknowledging the excited cheers of the crowd this very

Belfasts Great Northern Train Station

important couple is whisked through the welcoming doors of the Europa Hotel.

Older people in the crowd remembered that, years ago, there had stood on the site of this gleaming Europa Hotel a very different, but equally charming, building. The magnificent Grosvenor Rooms had represented, for so long in the early years of the twentieth century, the epitome of the high life in the unpretentious capital city of Northern Ireland. As their thoughts wandered back on this late twentieth century afternoon to that earlier, more sedate and serene age, their reverie was disturbed as they witnessed the arrival of arguably the most powerful person in the world. The time for daydreaming was over; anticipation had turned

Crowds line the streets of Belfast city centre. It is late on a dreary November afternoon in 1995. As the people anticipate the arrival of their visitor, they turn around and see the best known hotel edifice in the whole of Belfast, if not in northern Ireland – the Hastings

into the precincts of the hotel. Two people emerge, a man and a woman. The special visitors everyone has been waiting to see have arrived. They crane their necks to catch a glimpse and wave. A President of the United States of America is in town. After acknowledging the excited cheers of the crowd this very important

Chapter 1

Railways and Hotels – Tourism Springs to Life

Crowds line the streets of Belfast city centre. It is late on a dreary November afternoon in 1995. The light is fast fading. As the people anticipate the arrival of their visitor, they turn around and see the best known hotel edifice in the whole of Belfast, if not in Northern Ireland – the Hastings Europa Hotel. Their trance-like state is suddenly broken as a screaming motorcade swings round the corner of Howard Street into the normally bustling thoroughfare of Great Victoria Street – Belfast's Golden Mile. The unwieldy bullet-proof stretch limousine comes to a halt outside the hotel. Trench-coated bodyguards jump out of the car and into the precincts of the hotel. Two people emerge, a man and a woman. The special visitors everyone has been waiting to see have arrived. They crane their necks to catch a glimpse as the couple turn and wave. A President of the United States of America is in town. After acknowledging the excited cheers of the crowd this very important couple is whisked through the welcoming doors of the Europa Hotel.

Older people in the crowd remembered that, years ago, there had stood on the site of this gleaming Europa Hotel a very different, but equally charming, building. The magnificent Grosvenor Rooms had represented, for so long in the early years of the twentieth century, the epitome of the high life in the unpretentious capital city of Northern Ireland. As their thoughts wandered back on this late 20th-century afternoon to that earlier, more sedate and serene age, their reverie was disturbed as they witnessed the arrival of arguably the most powerful person in the world. The time for daydreaming was over; anticipation had turned to reality; President Bill Clinton was in town.

It seemed appropriate that the President had chosen the Europa as his base to signal the rebirth of Belfast and Northern Ireland. It was the opportune moment to copper fasten the wavering peace process. The Europa Hotel had, after all, been at the centre of practically every political, social and economic development for nearly 30 years.

When the Northern Ireland parliament was prorogued in 1972 by Edward Heath's government, much political discourse effectively moved from Stormont's debating chambers to the bars and restaurants of the Europa, especially the Beefeater and the lobby area outside it. Dialogue took place there between prominent Unionists and the new boys of the SDLP. Visiting politicians from Westminster and the United States mixed with the media personnel congregated there, for the Europa had become the perfect place to be briefed. This was particularly so when the British and Irish governments made their first attempt to kick-start politics again by holding the December 1973 Sunningdale conference.

The Europa had become home to many national and international journalists, many of whom have since become household names – Sir Max Hastings, Sir Trevor McDonald, Kate Adie, Jeremy Paxman, Conor O'Clery, John Simpson to name but a few.

During the early 1970s the existence of the Europa and its amenities made it possible for political parties, for the first time, to run large scale party conferences which they had hitherto been unable to arrange because of the dearth of suitable accommodation. From these beginnings emerged a new and more modern type of political organisation with a strong PR image to impress journalists and television reporters alike.

The influence of the Europa went well beyond politics. Along with quality restaurant developments on the Golden Mile, it was in the forefront of modernising the city by the introduction of London style entertainment which was particularly important to the business community in their efforts to attract investment. Visiting business people could now expect accommodation and entertainment on a par with the best that Britain could offer.

Great Northern Railway Terminus in Belfast (1934)

Also attracted to the hotel were many top international stars of film and stage, including Brad Pitt and Julia Roberts. Pitt, for example, checked into the Europa when he was researching his role for the movie *The Devil's Own*. In order to pick up the Belfast accent, he donned his sunglasses, sat in the hotel foyer and listened to staff and customers.

The Europa became the symbol of Belfast's rebirth. At that time, however, Northern Ireland's licensing laws were positively archaic with hotel bars in Belfast having to close at 10 p.m. Its owners, Grand Metropolitan, insisted on an extension to opening hours to ensure the hotel's success by bringing it into line with the other parts of the United Kingdom. They pressurised the then Minister, William Craig, into liberalising the law by permitting alcohol to be served on Sundays with main meals, and opened the door for a general relaxation of the interpretation of what constituted a 'main meal'. Consequently the Northern Ireland government passed the necessary reforms which not only pleased the Europa's owners but also everyone else in the licensed trade who were relieved to see this further normalisation of the once overregulated and restrictive licensing laws.

Not long after reopening under Hastings' ownership, the Europa was the venue for a major economic summit held by the British government on the future development of the Northern Ireland economy – the 1994 Northern Ireland Economic Summit hosted by the then Prime Minister, John Major. This conference was the biggest-ever in Northern Ireland and was made possible because of the Europa's extensive facilities. It was the only venue capable of accommodating, feeding and refreshing several hundred people in the one place. It led to investment announcements including the decision by Fujitsu to expand in Northern Ireland.

The story of the Europa Hotel is essentially the story of Northern Ireland over the past 30 years. The book tells the story of the hotel through the eyes of those who worked and stayed there.

Railways and Hotels

The genesis of the present day Europa Hotel lies in its location on Great Victoria Street in Belfast at the time of the emergence of rail travel. In 1839, the first steam trains began their journeys from Belfast to Lisburn and beyond and, just a year later in 1840, a splendid new railway terminus station was built for the Great Northern Railway Company precisely where the hotel stands today. The station was the design of the Ulster Railway's chief engineer, John Godwin, and was one of the city's most outstanding buildings for many years - until it was eventually replaced by the Europa Hotel in the early 1970s.

The station's wonderful *porte cochère* was added in 1891 in order to shelter the passengers under its protective cover as they climbed down from their horse-drawn carriages. The existence of the celebrated restaurant in the Grosvenor Rooms within the station complex also established a tradition of quality catering on the site.

The emergence of the railways – and it was not long before the entire island was covered by the steam railway system – also stimulated hotel development. The Belfast and County Down Railway built the luxurious Slieve Donard Hotel in Newcastle which opened its doors in June 1898. This hotel is still one of the Hastings Group's deluxe hotels to this day. The Great Northern Railway developed two plush hotels at Warrenpoint and Rostrevor and the Belfast and Northern Counties Railway built their magnificent hotel at Portrush.

Great Northern Railway Station, Great Victoria Street, Belfast (circa 1894)

Joyce and Norman Topley, two senior railwaymen born in the early twentieth century – and enthusiasts to this day – remembered the hustle and bustle at the station especially at holiday times when so many extra trains had to be scheduled. It was a hive of activity and was what made life on the railways an interesting and exciting one. By the mid 1930s, the hotels were absorbed by the Northern Ireland government when they decided to amalgamate rail and road transport to eliminate the intense competition that had been undermining passenger safety. The Northern Ireland Road Transport Board (NIRTB) was formed in 1935 and survived the Second World War – but only just. It was replaced by the Ulster Transport Authority (UTA) which immediately recommended savage cuts in the rail system and, with precious little debate or public consultation, proceeded to close many of the lines.

By January 1950, the majority of track, which had been in

existence in many cases for almost a century, was hastily and unceremoniously ripped up. The only lines to remain were the Belfast to Dublin service, a journey then of around two and a half hours, which today takes almost as long in the high profile Enterprise express; the line from Belfast to Bangor; the boat-train to Larne and the Belfast to Londonderry service linking Coleraine and Portrush.

One important symbol of the once great rail system remained. The GNR terminus on Great Victoria Street still had its role to play in the much-reduced rail network. The trains from Belfast to Dublin continued to run and, for the next twenty years, the magic of that much-loved building remained. By the late 1960s, however, the death knell for this magnificent building was sounded as the government of Terence O'Neill opted for its own version of 'out with the old and in with the new'. The GNR station and the Grosvenor Rooms were to be demolished to make way for that icon on the revitalised Belfast townscape – the Europa Hotel. And with the demise of the Grosvenor Rooms the government also put the UTA hotels on the market.

July 1971

The Birth of the Europa

In 1966 the chairman of the Ulster Transport Authority (UTA), Arthur Algeo, announced that, following their recent sale of the six UTA hotels to Grand Metropolitan Hotels Limited, they would build a brand new hotel on a site in Great Victoria Street.

It had been one of the conditions of the sale of the existing hotels that a new hotel be built. Planning permission was soon granted for the construction of a hotel with 200 bedrooms and five suites, each with its own private bathroom, a first for any hotel in Northern Ireland. It was hoped that building would start by the beginning of 1968. Farrans of Dunmurry won the contract to build the hotel and Messrs. Sidney Kaye, Eric Firkin and Partners of London were appointed as architects. The work eventually commenced in the autumn of 1969. Grand Metropolitan chairman, Maxwell Joseph, declared that such a hotel was greatly needed in Belfast and thus the idea of the Europa Hotel was conceived.

For nearly two years the citizens of Belfast looked on as the massive structure of the hotel gradually reached its impressive height

of twelve storeys. At the time it was the tallest building in Belfast city centre and represented a £2 million investment (at today's prices around £20 million). The city had been in the doldrums since the 1950s until Captain Terence O'Neill, Prime Minister of Northern Ireland from 1963 until 1969, determined that a rather dreary Belfast should be transformed and modernised. And what better way to do this than by having a first class hotel in the midst of the capital city. No longer would Belfast be described as 'small, dull, dreary and sad'. The Europa would show the world that Belfast and Northern Ireland were ready and able to attract new visitors and enterprises. On 18 December 1970 the 'topping out' ceremony took place, performed by Harper Brown, the man who was to be the hotel's first general manager. The hotel opened its doors for its first guests in July 1971.

A Developing and Expanding Economy

The concept of the Europa Hotel was born amid the optimism of the late 1960s which had seen major inward investment from multi-national corporations in Belfast and throughout Northern Ireland. Industrial production in the sixties, especially in the Belfast

New Hotel for Belfast city center

area, had grown faster than anywhere else within the United Kingdom. Northern Ireland had become the European centre of man-made fibre production following substantial investment from Courtaulds, ICI and British Enkalon. Ford-Autolite and

Grundig had set up plants at Dunmurry. Harland and Wolff had won a series of orders for large tankers and attracted the interest of the shipping magnates, Aristotle Onassis and Fred Olsen. The aircraft firm of Short Brothers and Harland, under the

leadership of Sir Philip Foreman, was winning orders for its new Skyvan freighters and was developing the prototype of their revolutionary vertical take-off Harrier jump jet. By 1966 unemployment had been slashed to just 5.5%. Although this boom was only to

New Hotel

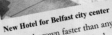

For your own comfort,

It had been one of the conditions

work eventually commenced in the autumn of 1969. Grand Metropolitan chairman, Maxwell

Chapter 2

The Birth of the Europa

In 1966 the chairman of the Ulster Transport Authority (UTA), Arthur Algeo, announced that, following their recent sale of the six UTA hotels to Grand Metropolitan Hotels Limited, they would build a brand new hotel on a site in Great Victoria Street. It had been one of the conditions of the sale of the existing hotels that a new hotel be built. Planning permission was soon granted for the construction of a hotel with 200 bedrooms and five suites, each with its own private bathroom, a first for any hotel in Northern Ireland. It was hoped that building would start by the beginning of 1968. Farrans of Dunmurry won the contract to build the hotel and Messrs. Sidney Kaye, Eric Firkin and Partners of London were appointed as architects. The work eventually commenced in the autumn of 1969. Grand Metropolitan chairman, Maxwell Joseph, declared that such a hotel was greatly needed in Belfast and thus the idea of the Europa Hotel was conceived.

Europa Belfast
Europa Hotel

For nearly two years the citizens of Belfast looked on as the massive structure of the hotel gradually reached its impressive height of twelve storeys. At the time it was the tallest building in Belfast city centre and represented a £2

million investment (at today's prices around £20 million). The city had been in the doldrums since the 1950s until Captain Terence O'Neill, Prime Minister of Northern Ireland from 1963 until 1969, determined that a rather dreary Belfast should be transformed and modernised. What better way to do this than by having a first class hotel in the midst of the capital city? No longer would Belfast be described as 'small, dull, dreary and sad'. The Europa would show the world that Belfast and Northern Ireland were ready and able to attract new visitors and enterprises. On 18 December 1970 the traditional end-of-construction 'topping out' ceremony took place, performed by Harper Brown, the man who was to be the hotel's first general manager. The hotel opened its doors for the first guests in July 1971.

A Developing and Expanding Economy

The concept of the Europa Hotel was born amid the optimism of the late 1960s which had seen major inward investment from multi-national corporations in Belfast and throughout Northern Ireland. Industrial production in the sixties, especially in the Belfast area, had grown faster than anywhere else within the United Kingdom. Northern Ireland had become the European centre of man-made fibre production following substantial investment from Courtaulds, ICI and British Enkalon. Ford-Autolite and Grundig had set up plants at Dunmurry. Harland and Wolff had won a series of orders for large tankers and attracted the interest of the shipping magnates, Aristotle Onassis and Fred Olsen. The aircraft firm of Short Brothers and Harland, under the leadership of Sir Philip Foreman, was winning orders for its new Skyvan freighters and was developing the prototype of their revolutionary vertical take-off Harrier jump jet. By 1966 unemployment had been slashed to just 5.5%. Although this boom was only to last for less than a decade,

nonetheless it seemed a fortuitous time for the opening of the Europa.

The Hotel's Style and Design

From the beginning the Europa was destined to be special. Its style was terrific compared with the old Grand Central and Midland Hotels, neither of which even had en suite bathrooms. They had been commercial travellers' hotels and had become very run-down.

Maxwell Joseph's message to new staff, July 1971

The design of the hotel, too, was exceptional, if not revolutionary – for Belfast at least. A curved tower bedroom block was built on top of a ground and first floor podium. Bedrooms, apart from being en suite, boasted private telephones and black and white television sets. There were single and double rooms as well as a small number of two roomed suites. The cost of a single room per night was £4.75 and £8 for a double room, with suites

from the Chairman to you

You have joined one of the largest Hotel and Catering Groups in the World, and certainly the most progressive. We are proud of our achievements and are determined that we shall always maintain the highest standards in our relations with both our guests and our staff.

This, your booklet, explains how we work and also sets out briefly the guidelines we have adopted to achieve smooth operation. It also tells you of the special benefits and privileges which are extended to members of our Grand Met. "family", and of certain special rewards which are given for extra effort.

Please read your booklet carefully. If there is anything you do not understand, your immediate Head of Department or Personnel Manager will be glad to explain it.

We are pleased to have you with us, and hope that you will be happy.

Sincerely,

The Europa under construction, 1971

various companies which sponsored them. There were the 'Guinness', the 'Bass', the 'Powers', the 'Bushmills' and the 'Benson and Hedges' paddocks, and each was attended by its own dedicated member of staff. Covering the floor was a straw coloured carpet and the ceiling was decorated with world famous racing colours. A new beer, 'Europa Bass Ale', was ceremoniously unveiled to celebrate the opening of the bar. Journalist Chris Ryder, who worked for Bass at the time, remembered the brown boxes from Worthington's Ale which were brought in and placed on the counter in front of the pumps. This was the kind of prestige which the hotel revelled in during its early days.

The bar soon became a meeting place for many local people who came just to gaze and marvel at the hotel's luxurious surroundings. The splendour of the Europa's trappings offered a stunning contrast to the plainness of their own working class local pubs in other parts of the city.

The hotel, of course, had attractive restaurants. The Beefeater, similar to the one in the Clifton Ford in London, reached by the spiral staircase from the foyer, was situated on the first floor. Its customers were pampered by the attentive hostesses in regulation Grand Metropolitan beefeater style uniforms and then tempted with menus offering the finest continental food. It even provided more local fare for the less gastronomically adventurous. The head chef, Norman Owen, who had come from a prestigious London hotel, considered that Northern Ireland people were 'rather conservative' when it came to dining. He was determined to educate the locals and persuade them to try something a little different. Early examples of 1971-72 menus are shown on the next page.

A typical bill for two diners, which included four courses followed by coffee and liqueurs, came to around £9. This

costing less than £20. A continental breakfast was also included. The rooms also had plush green and brown curtains and gold bedspreads – the standard Grand Metropolitan livery and similar to the Europa in Brussels and the Clifton Ford in London. When the first guests arrived during July 1971 they could, aside from relaxing in their sumptuous sleeping accommodation, sample the delights of the hotel's other facilities. The opening function was a splendid banquet held on 20 July 1971 for the members of the Ulster Flying Club and their guests.

The Whip and Saddle was the public bar. It became a very popular place especially for journalists who frequented the hotel in the early 1970s. Several drinking 'paddocks', like snugs but with higher white walls, were named after the

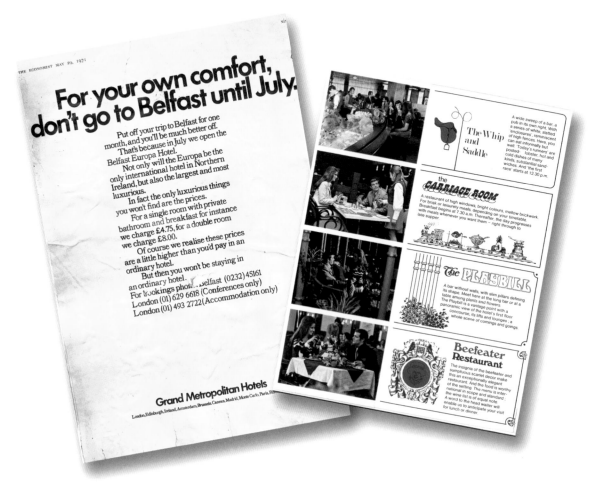

was considered, for the time, to be on the expensive side when the average weekly wage in the early 1970s was £12, but more than reasonable for such luxurious surroundings, smooth assured service and top class cooking.

It was not long before the aptly named Penthouse Rooftop restaurant opened, affording the most magnificent views all over the city from 180 feet above the ground. It gave the kind of romance to eating and drinking which Belfast had not previously known. There was dancing at the weekends for the daring and

adventurous. The first floor Playbill cocktail bar was situated next door to the Beefeater restaurant. On the ground floor there was the Carriage Room, a large coffee shop which had enormous windows overlooking Great Victoria Street. Not only was the new Europa the place to be, it was also the place to be seen.

Another innovation at the Europa was the

Menu 25 £3·00	Menu 26 £3·25
Pineapple Boat	Cornets of Smoked Salmon Caribbean (*palm hearts rolled in smoked salmon with a piquant sauce*)
+ + +	+ + +
Turtle Soup with Sherry	Consommé with Sherry
+ + +	+ + +
Entrecôte Steak Valentin (*grilled sirloin steak with a light Madeira sauce, pimentos, and tomatoes*)	Fillet of Beef Wellington (*whole bunched fillets of beef wrapped in puff pastry with shallots and mushrooms*)
Medley of Peas and Carrots	Cauliflower Mornay
Parmentier Potatoes	Parisienne Potatoes
+ + +	+ + +
Eclaire Maxine (*a puff pastry flan filled with maraschino-soaked sponge, strawberry preserve and cream, decorated with almonds and served with vanilla ice cream*)	Omelette Surprise Europa
+ + +	+ + +
Petit Fours	Petit Fours
+ + +	+ + +
Coffee	Coffee

presence of a superb conference and banqueting suite. Up to 700 people could be seated for a conference and over 400 for a dinner or luncheon. The names given to this floor reflected Ireland's New York connections with its Manhattan, Madison and Lexington areas. In an early advertisement for the conference facilities, Grand Metropolitan described the Europa as a 'conference hotel extraordinary'; where a conference 'can be handled with aplomb' and whose facilities were 'infinitely versatile'.

The Penthouse Poppets

For some, however, the Europa will be best remembered, especially in its early days, for its Penthouse Poppets. They were to be found on the 12th floor of the hotel in the Penthouse Night Club. The Poppets were the Europa's version of the Bunny Girls who worked in the more upmarket London establishments. The first young women asked to become Poppets had absolutely no idea what a Poppet was. One of the original Poppets described how she found out what she was expected to do. She was to be dressed, somewhat scantily, in the best French velvet costume and her duties were principally to pay close attention to her customers in the club. She was to dance and sing and become a general all-round entertainer.

The Poppets became an instant success with their eye-catching routines and they undoubtedly awakened a very puritanical Belfast from its slumber. The city had never known anything like them before. The girls thought the club was a happy place to work and they certainly attracted crowds to the hotel, especially at weekends. There may have been vacancies for staff members from time to time but never for the position of Penthouse Poppet. They represented a symbol of life and hope and became little short of an institution in the otherwise drab surroundings of a city under siege.

THE PENTHOUSE

The Europa's own nightclub.
High above the city.
The most sophisticated scene in town,
you wine and dine superbly,
dancing as and when you will. Book a table.
Take the lift to the great night out.

Another extract from a marketing brochure showing The Penthouse nightclub

One former Poppet, Evelyn Sullivan, who worked at the Europa from 1972 until 1975, recalled how very expensive and exclusive the Penthouse was. A Coke cost £1 (about £6 today) and a beer £1.20 (over £7) and Evelyn remembered that some of the young men would club together to buy a few Cokes or beers just to say that they had been there! Evelyn and the other 10 Poppets, who included Liz Rogers, Alice McHugh (later to become Miss Northern Ireland) and Sue Porter, were each paid £4 (£25) but they could often earn a further £16 (around £100) in tips – an excellent payment for a good night's work. During the 1974 Ulster Workers' Council strike, the Poppets worked

Harper Brown – the Europa's first General Manager

'Charismatic' and 'a perfectionist' were the words which described the man who drove the Europa forward in its early days. Harper Brown's name was synonymous with the hotel in the 1970s. From the beginning he lived and breathed the hotel. During the hotel's darkest days there were weeks when Harper never left the premises. He preferred to be where 'the action' was. Always seen as a 'front of house' person, Harper Brown thoroughly enjoyed meeting and greeting all his guests. Although he did occasionally live in the family home on the outskirts of Belfast, Harper and his wife, Sally, had their home in an apartment on the eighth floor of the hotel. (Harper had met his wife, who came from near Letterkenny in County Donegal, when they both were working in the Grand Central Hotel in Belfast and they were married in 1949).

By the time Grand Metropolitan appointed him as general manager in 1971, Harper Brown had been in the hotel business for twenty five years. From his earliest days at home in Dervock, County Antrim, Harper seemed destined to work in the catering industry. He had learnt how to cook and bake from his mother and, after his education at Belfast Royal Academy, he first went to work, in 1946, aged 18, in the Grand Central Hotel in Belfast's Royal Avenue. There he worked as a trainee and grew to love the hotel trade. He pursued his career in England where he was appointed to the staff of the Grand and the Queen's Hotels in Birmingham before moving to the Adelphi in Liverpool. He subsequently moved on to the Charing Cross Hotel in London and then to the Royal Victoria in Sheffield.

In 1956 he returned to Northern Ireland to run his own catering business. After three years, however, the draw of the hotel business proved too much for him. Accepting his brother Thomson's proposal to act as relief manager in

Harper Brown, the General Manager, with a Penthouse Poppet

by candlelight and, as Evelyn recalled, they even served some of the strike leaders. After all, the Europa never closed!

Harper Brown, General Manager 1971 - 1985

Harper Brown became an institution in the Europa. Everybody knew him and everybody liked him. He took as much time in getting to know the boy who delivered the papers each day as he did in meeting some very important guest to the hotel. Although he was a tough man to work for, his staff always admired his determination and resolve. The hotel was 'Harper's baby'. When the television journalist, Bernard Falk, spoke of Harper Brown in 1973, he declared that he 'stood up to the bombers no matter what else'.

In 1975, Harper was awarded the MBE for his services to the hotel industry and for his tenacity in the face of over twenty bombs and many more bomb hoaxes.

The Original Staff Team

Here we recall those magnificent members of staff who worked in the Europa in its early days. Many of them had transferred from other Grand Metropolitan hotels in London, and they brought with them their experience and expertise to the company's new Belfast location. The fact that they came from various foreign countries such as the Lebanon, Egypt and a number of European countries added to the international flavour of the new Europa.

The **house manager**, in charge of everything except the catering, was 24 year old Matthew Sherlock from County Donegal. His assistant was Bob Newton who came from Yorkshire.

The first **catering manager** was the aptly

the Northern Counties Hotel in Portrush, Harper gladly took up the position and, before long, he became general manager of the City Hotel in Londonderry. He was then appointed to the Midland Hotel in Belfast where he remained until 1967. In 1968 he was appointed to the management team of Grand Metropolitan Hotels who wanted him as their general manager of the newly conceived Europa Hotel. By way of training and preparation, therefore, he spent three years managing two of London's famous hotels, Fleming's and the Grosvenor Victoria.

Harper Brown, MBE

The Europa staff celebrating the hotel's 3rd birthday in July 1974

named 26 year old Christopher Cook. He had also worked in London but was glad to be able to accept the challenge at the Europa.

Norman Owen, the **chef de cuisine**, had come over from England with his family. In 1972, he became the first recipient of the title of Cook/Chef of the Year – an honour which reflected very favourably on the Europa itself. After three years in his post at the Europa, Norman was appointed to the post of catering adviser for the Hastings Hotels Group – a position he held for a period

before returning to work in England. His deputy, Bernard Blake, succeeded Norman as chef de cuisine. Other members of the **kitchen** staff included Bernard Hughes, Maurice Price, Gerry Burns, Jim Leckey and Eamon Rosato.

The husband and wife team of Georges and Janet Hamon were **reception manager** and **hotel manageress** of the **Carriage Room** respectively. Georges was from Brittany and his wife, whom he met whilst they were both working at the Mayfair Hotel in London, was English. They had married just before coming to Belfast.

A young German, Egon Kahnert, had been employed as **restaurant manager**. He had previously worked in

Switzerland, Paris and London and was, therefore, a most experienced member of the first Europa team. He had been such a popular manager in the Britannia Hotel in London that he brought many of his colleagues over to Belfast with him.

Other members of the staff team at that time included the **banqueting manager,** Ivor Walsh and the **public relations officer,** Lynn Stewart, who spent much of her early time advertising the hotel and assisting the **sales manager**, Anthony Fudge. The **housekeeping** team was led by Sally Brown, Harper's wife.

Rae McParland and Stanley Rowan ran the **'Whip and Saddle'** bar serving, amongst others, the many journalists who were resident in the Europa during the 1970s and 1980s. Paul Christie was the **'Playbill'** bar manager.

The first **training manager** was Gareth Jones. Apart from the builders, he was one of only four staff members in post when the hotel opened - Harper Brown, Eileen Carson, his secretary, and **purchasing officer**, Sam McVeigh, being the other three. Gareth worked closely with Harper Brown and spent many of his early days with Grand Metropolitan travelling around their hotels helping staff become accustomed to decimalisation which had also been introduced in 1971.

Jennifer McLornan, Sandie Delargy (whose husband, Danny, was also on the staff), Carole McCrea, Ruby Black and Patricia Docherty were on the **reception** staff in the early 1970s. Philip Drennan was **banqueting manager** and the **banqueting head waiter** was Robert Kerr.

The redoubtable Jimmy Connor was the **head porter** from the early days in 1972. He and his team worked closely with a sometimes excitable Harper Brown to retain calm in the Europa at a time when bomb scares were an everyday occurrence. Although the Europa was then the 'sick man' of the Grand Metropolitan Group, nonetheless the directors of the company, and Maxwell Joseph himself, were friendly employers, although, as Jimmy recalled, none of them ever actually stayed overnight in Belfast. As an honoured member of the 'Les Clefs d'Or' organisation, Jimmy regularly attended their meetings in various Irish venues and, on one occasion, hosted their gathering at the Europa itself. Jimmy clearly recalls the events of the Ulster Workers' Council strike in May 1974. Harper Brown was, coincidentally, on holiday and Jimmy and the rest of the staff had to 'hold the fort'. Whilst all other hotels were shut down, the Europa did not close. The strikers' leaders shrewdly realised that, if they wanted coverage in the newspapers, they needed journalists to write their daily reports and, as the world's pressmen were staying in the Europa, then they would not order it to be closed down. And so it remained open for the duration. One of the London reporters wrote to Maxwell Joseph at the end of the strike commending the excellent work of all the staff in the hotel and he quickly and positively responded by awarding everyone a £5 bonus in their next wage packet!

Top to Bottom, Mat Sherlock, Chris Cook, Norman Owen, George Hamon, Egon Kahert and Ivor Walsh

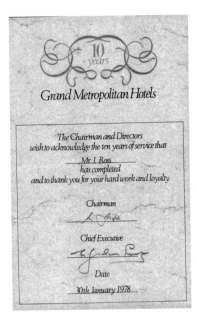

The **head hall porter** was Tommy Dunne and Micky Carson was one of his porters. Jimmy Ross, who had been transferred from the Midland Hotel, was the **cloakroom attendant**. One of the original **maintenance** team was George Cooper and the **storeman** was Joe Doran.

A number of staff joined the Europa team soon after the opening, including Paddy McAnerney, Roy Bolton, Alistair McCracken, Richard Wilson, George Scobbie, Glynis Messom, David Storey, Peter Woolnough, Stewart Decotts, John Sloan, Pim Dalm and David Craig. During the early days, too, there were at least four weddings amongst members of the Europa staff.

The hotel was soon employing over one hundred staff, both full and part-time and all of them trained at Grand Metropolitan's training centre based at the Laharna Hotel in Larne. New staff recruited from outside Northern Ireland also had to apply for a work permit to enable them to work at the hotel. They found it strange to be considered as aliens! The team was up and running and ready for any possible challenge. But the challenge which faced them was to be an epic and difficult struggle, far beyond what even the most pessimistic person could have predicted.

Jimmy Ross, hotel porter, and the certificate he received for 10 years of service

Great Victoria Street was regularly flooded until the early 1970s as it is situated on top of the river Blackstaff. Very deep piles had to be driven into the river bed to ensure sound foundations for the Europa Note the bus, with the Europa under construction in the background, bravely attempting to continue its regular route through the flood waters.
(from a contemporary newspaper)

Selection of early Europa memorabilia including brochures, menus and wine lists

Chapter Three

August 1971

Printed in

The Crossroads of Intrigue

A month after Harper Brown had welcomed the first guests the Northern Ireland Prime Minister, Brian Faulkner, introduced internment. It was an abject failure and Northern Ireland erupted into violence on a scale that had never been seen before.

Guests looking out from the top floor windows could see clear evidence of the orgies of violence crippling Belfast. They witnessed tracer bullets and burning barricades. Newly arrived customers had barely opened their cases in their bedrooms when the bombers go to work – and with a vengeance. Within a month of opening the hotel was hit by a bomb which caused considerable damage, destroying the restaurant and the kitchens. The violence effectively emptied the Europa before it had time to fill.

The Europa Hotel was an attractive target. It was a symbol of Government policy of bringing new life to Belfast and was easily accessible, situated right in the

Trevor McDonald, in the centre of the picture, runs across Great Victoria Street shortly after a bomb explosion

heart of the city. The bomb had, from the IRA's standpoint, the desired effect of plenty of press coverage. Many guests quickly packed their bags and did not return for a very long time, although the more determined did stay and simply asked for

their rooms to be vacuumed and the curtains drawn. For most of the early 1970s the hotels main customers were journalists from all over the world who had come to report on the increasing violence in Northern Ireland.

Throughout Northern Ireland nearly 700 people were to die in terrorist incidents over the next year and a half. There were countless bombs which either went off in the hotel or exploded near enough to cause considerable damage. In one week alone

in 1974, the hotel had been twice "flambéed" by the provisional IRA. Once the terrorists even calmly walked into the hotel and left their device near the lift shafts with the word "IRA" scribbled on it. They did not want anyone to be in doubt as to

Security Tightened

Guests looking out from the top floor windows could see clear evidence of the orgies of violence witnessed

The Europa Hotel was an attractive target. It was a symbol of Government policy of bringing new life to Belfast and was easily accessible, situated right in the bomb had,

tomers were journalists from all over the world who had come to report on the increasing violence in Northern Ireland.

Throughout Northern Ireland nearly 700 people were to die in the next

Chapter 3

The Crossroads of Intrigue

The Fleet Street of Belfast

A month after Harper Brown had welcomed the first guests the Northern Ireland Prime Minister, Brian Faulkner, introduced internment. It was an abject failure and Northern Ireland erupted into violence on a scale that had never been seen before. Guests looking out from the top floor windows could see clear evidence of the orgies of violence crippling Belfast. They witnessed tracer bullets and burning barricades. Newly arrived customers had barely opened their cases in their bedrooms when the bombers got to work – and with a vengeance. Within a month of opening the hotel was hit by a bomb which caused considerable damage, destroying the restaurant and the kitchens. The violence effectively emptied the Europa before it had time to fill.

The Europa Hotel was an attractive target. It was a symbol of Government policy of bringing new life to Belfast and was easily accessible, situated right in the heart of the city. The bomb had, from the IRA's standpoint, the desired effect of plenty of press coverage. Many guests quickly packed their bags and did not return for a very long time, although the more determined did stay and simply asked for their rooms to be vacuumed and the curtains drawn. For most of the early 1970s the hotels main customers were journalists from all over the world who had come to report on the increasing violence in Northern Ireland.

Throughout Northern Ireland nearly 700 people were to die in terrorist incidents over the next year and a half. There were countless bombs which either went off in the hotel or exploded near enough to cause considerable damage. In one week alone in 1974, the hotel was twice *flambéed* by the provisional IRA. Once the terrorists even calmly walked into the hotel and left their device near the lift shafts with the word "IRA" scribbled on it. They did not want anyone to be in doubt as to who had left the package.

Courage in the face of adversity

The Europa staff carried on, cleared the glass and continued as best they could. Harper Brown would not close the hotel or let the IRA get on top of his staff and himself. Occasionally he displayed what some saw as courage and others rank foolishness. The story was once told that he picked up a parcel which the IRA had left in the hotel and took it outside. The terrorists then brought the device back inside only for the fearless Harper to take it out for a second time. The IRA men had met their match and fled the scene.

Sadly the grim story of Northern Ireland in general and of the Europa in particular changed little for years. For some considerable period, the Province and the hotel shared the unenviable reputation of being the most bombed place

Trevor McDonald, in the centre of the picture, runs across Great Victoria Street shortly after a bomb explosion

anywhere in the world. There were many acts of pure heroism attaching to events in the hotel. The distinguished head of the Army bomb disposal squad at the time was Major George Styles who was regularly called upon to make safe some of the most dangerous bombs which had ever been constructed. In October 1972 he was sent to the Europa to disarm two anti-handling bombs. These were the type of devices which were set to explode as soon as they were touched. It took him seven hours to defuse one of the bombs and he completed this all too delicate task just a couple of days after a friend and a colleague of his had been killed trying to make safe a similar device.

On occasions such as this, an ever grateful Harper Brown brought out the champagne for the men involved in that most desperate of duties. Major Styles was awarded the George Cross for his bravery, the highest commendation the Army can give in peacetime. His citation read "that on two occasions Major Styles placed himself at great personal risk to minimise the damage to the rest of his disposal team'. Years later George Styles G.C. returned to the Europa, as a civilian, to launch his autobiography *Bombs have no Pity* and by way of showing their appreciation a grateful Europa staff rolled out the red carpet.

On 3 May 1974, two massive explosions rocked the Europa causing yet more damage. At around 5p.m. a bomb went off in one of the water tanks on the top floor, quickly affecting all levels of the hotel. One hour later a gas main was ruptured on the ground floor, filling the entire foyer with fumes. As ever the hotel staff showed their defiance as they efficiently dealt with the crisis. It is remarkable that in all the many explosions in or near the hotel, only two or three people were slightly injured. Incredibly no one was ever killed. This miracle was partly due to the speed with which the staff evacuated the premises. On occasions the hotel had hundreds of guests inside the building and it was cleared in less than twenty minutes.

On one occasion, Carolyn Stalker, the front office manager noticed a suspicious truck in front of the hotel. There had been no warning but she decided that the guests and staff should be immediately evacuated. This process took less than 15 minutes whereupon the truck exploded. Had Carolyn not used her intuition, many people would surely have been killed or injured. By lunchtime that same day everyone was back to work, notwithstanding the huge hole in the side of the hotel.

Sadly, however, the worst of the Troubles was epitomised by the story of a popular character and Jewish businessman, Lennie Kaitcher. He owned an antique jewellery concession shop in the foyer of the Europa in the 1970s and was well-known to all the staff in the hotel and much respected by all who knew him. In the late 1970s he was abducted from the Europa and subsequently murdered after which time many of the strong Jewish community left Belfast.

The hotel's windows had to be boarded up many times due to frequent bomb explosions and, for a time, the Europa became known as 'Hardboard Hotel'

Harper Brown's
specially commissioned
Europa Hotel tie

primary task of keeping the hotel open. Harper's motto was 'we never close'. He insisted that staff continued to serve drinks to their equally determined customers even though they were sitting under umbrellas in the bar. In the words of journalist Martin Dillon, it was "through the quixotic personality of Harper Brown, that the Europa became a symbol of defiance and determination to survive the ravages of a war torn city". So important was the Europa as the City's only significant meeting place that it became known as the "Parliament". MPs from all shades of political opinion met there on a regular basis. The Europa was a beleaguered Northern Ireland's link to the outside world.

Incredibly, meals were prepared to an exceptionally high standard in the kitchens which very often had themselves been hit by an explosion. During the days of the 1974 Ulster Workers' Council (UWC) strike when there was no electric power, the inventive chef and his staff lit a fire in the yard outside the kitchens and from this unlikely source hotel guests were served up their usual delicious meal by candlelight, completely unaware of where it had been cooked. John Simpson, now the BBC's international editor, writing about the Europa in his memoirs *A Mad World, My Master* recalls "At the Europa Hotel the most bombed hotel in the world, they kept the night club going throughout the 1970s as though they were in the South of France, and the kitchen provided excellent room service only twenty minutes

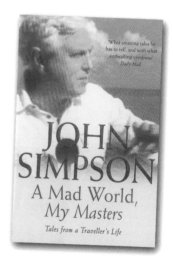

Parliament's New Home

Harper Brown stuck to their

Kim Tomlinson, Miss Belfast Europa 1980

after each new bomb scare".

The hotel was determined to survive. And survive it did. It was many years before it eventually had to close to allow damage caused by an explosion to be repaired. The hotel became known as 'hardboard' hotel. Such was the probability, not the possibility, of the Europa being damaged in an explosion that a standing order with a window supplier was always in place. As soon as the windows were blown out in an explosion the glaziers arrived to replace them. Once the glass had been swept up by the hard-working staff, the repairers moved in. But, as often as not, the window frames themselves had been warped in the blast and therefore the replacement windows would not fit. So they had to revert to covering them with large pieces of hardboard. And so the name 'hardboard hotel' stuck to the increasingly shabby and forlorn building.

Yet in spite of so many stories of doom and gloom there were examples of much more normal events. In 1979 the *News Letter* journalist Sandra Chapman related that she had the pleasure of meeting the author, Colleen McCullough, who had chosen the Europa to publicise the sequel to her best selling novel, *The Thorn Birds*. Only later did Sandra and her clutch of journalists having lunch that day realise that they had been in the company of a potential legend.

Trevor McClintock, the managing director of the drinks firm of Gilbey's which was owned by Grand Metropolitan, remembers many major events which they sponsored in the 'Whip and Saddle' bar. The Smirnoff jazz band was a particularly popular attraction in the bar during the late 1970s and early 1980s enticing large Saturday afternoon crowds who, in the prevailing circumstances, would never normally have ventured into the city centre.

Northern Ireland's favourite boxing son was Barry McGuigan. Sponsored by Gilbey's and managed by Barney Eastwood of B.J.Eastwood of bookmaker fame, Barry's weigh-in for his British Featherweight title fight in 1983 took place in the Europa. TV boxing commentator, Harry Carpenter, described the scene to his national and international audiences from the hotel foyer which was thronged that evening with the great and the good from the world's boxing fraternity. When Barry subsequently won his fight, the whole city celebrated - and the Europa had shared in his glory. Barry later went on to become the WBA Featherweight champion of the world in 1985.

Harper Brown was always full of ideas. He decided that there should be some tangible recognition to those people who had stayed in the hotel through its darkest days. So he had a number of fine Irish poplin ties made in a pleasant shade of brown with the Europa motif emblazoned thereon in gold. He presented many of these ties over the years and together with the tie itself each recipient received a "citation" which read '…is authorised to wear the Belfast Europa tie which signifies that its owner was a valued guest at the hotel during the period from the summer of 1971 to the present date. The manager and his staff present the tie in recognition of the loyalty of their guests to the hotel during these unhappy days. We hope that the tie will be worn with pride as a memento of their stay and with assurance that its owner will always be welcomed back to enjoy the hotel both during the present Troubles and when peace returns'. The tie became a cherished possession. Harper also produced three other ties which were presented on special occasions to staff, to the Penthouse Poppets and to members of the Army bomb disposal squads.

There was also the annual Miss Belfast Europa contest which ran for many years; pictured here is the 1980 winner, Kim Tomlinson, outside the Penthouse Suite. She was an 18 year old typist who thus qualified for the Miss Grand Metropolitan Hotels contest in London.

There is no doubt that life for staff and customers at the Europa during the 1970s was difficult. Yet there remained a totally positive attitude to keeping the place open for the needs of those who used the hotel. The locals still came at the weekends for entertainment, and the journalists continued to flock to Belfast and to the Europa as much as ever. The hotel represented a kind of microcosm of life in Northern Ireland. It represented what was good and bad in the Province. Above all, its continuing presence defied the bomber and proved to a very wary public that it was there to stay.

When the hotel had reluctantly to close for three months at the end of 1976 after devastating bomb damage, there were rumours that it might close permanently and even reopen as a private hospital. But to show its continuing resolve, it opened again in a further show of defiance. By this time it was reputed that the Europa had been attacked 28 times although, despite every adversity, its high standards of housekeeping had always been maintained. Early in 1977 the hotel received a welcome boost following the unlikely announcement that a group of Belgian officials from the Royal Automobile Club of Belgium had secretly tested hotel conditions throughout the British Isles and the Belfast Europa had come out top.

Throughout the 1970s Grand Metropolitan continued to show faith in the Europa. There were no profits being made and newspaper reports and television programmes were not concerned with its fine food and comfortable accommodation, but with the attacks on the hotel by the resurgent IRA. The tourist trade in Northern Ireland during this decade was practically nonexistent and hotels were few and far between – at least those that were still open. Hotels in every town and village were being bombed including the new state-of-the-art Russell Court in Belfast which opened and then closed within two short years. The fact that the Europa remained open did, at least, give some semblance of normality for the few intrepid travellers who were determined to visit. They were, however, constantly reminded of the city's troubles every time they closed their bedroom door on which a permanent notice had been affixed. It reminded the visitor that 'because of the civil unrest in Belfast, they may have to speedily evacuate the building'.

A Crossroads of Intrigue

For many years the hotel's main customers were

Bomb No 29 This was the devastated foyer at Belfast's Europa Hotel after yesterday's bomb attack—the 29th the building has suffered in the I.R.A campaign. *Picture: FRED HOARE*

WAR OF NERVES

...y pushes back

The shattered front of the Belfast Europa Hotel damaged yesterday for the 26th time in the I.R.A. campaign of violence.

Blast No. 26 for the Europa

...staff in the Belfast Europa ...tel swung into a familiar ...ing-up routine yester-...day, less than an hour after ...the 26th bomb attack on the building.

Three terrorists drove up to the hotel in Great Victoria Street around 12-40 p.m. One stayed in the car — a red Cortina — while the other two...

He carried the suitcase to the back of the foyer and left it between the lift and the stairs. After shouting a warning, the terrorists ran back to their car and drove off.

The hotel and surrounding area...

...lb of explosive, caused extensive damage to the ground floor and the first floor bar but the other floors escaped damage.

Traffic was diverted from the area for nearly an hour after the explosion while soldiers searched the building for other devices.

But within minutes of the all-clear being given, workmen and members of the staff had started a big board-ing-up operation led by manager Mr. Harper Brown.

More than £1 million has been ...g bomb damage since ...n building opened in...

Boys dump bomb

DEATH BOOKS IN AT HOTEL

The box of death . . . standing in the Europa Hotel foyer last night journalists from all over the world who had come to report on the on-going trouble and strife in Northern Ireland. Had it not been for their business the hotel would not have survived. Many of these journalists have since become household names. There are few buildings in Europe which have produced so many stories and vivid recollections as the Europa. Their news and feature writing became the stuff of legend and their memories of their stay have lost nothing in the telling.

Simon Hoggart, *The Guardian*'s Belfast reporter from 1971 until 1973, describes the Europa as a 'headquarters, a training school, a private club and only marginally a hotel'. 'Everyone', he remembers, 'came to the Europa – the press mainly, but everyone else came because of the press. If you were a politician, or a soldier, or even a paramilitary, you knew that was where to put the word out. It was the information exchange'.

The main meeting place for the journalists, especially those from the broadsheet papers who tended to be sent over for stints and therefore stayed in the hotel, was the downstairs bar, the Whip and Saddle, known, for reasons lost in antiquity, as the 'Whip and Crutch'. This was the first port of call for reporters who needed to be filled in instantly on what was going on. If things seemed quiet someone would declare a public holiday which meant no one was allowed to do any work, unless of course, something really important happened. It was thought very bad form to send an article on such a day.

The restaurant had what seemed, to most journalists, the height of sophistication – at-table phones. If there was a call for you, the waiter brought a phone over and plugged it in. Sometimes it was a call to go off into the night to report on a shooting or a riot, in which case the staff would keep supper warm for the reporters. Conor O'Clery, now the international editor for *The Irish Times*

and during the 1970s their northern editor, remembers that it was a mark of a reporter's status to have the telephone trailing a long lead, brought by a waiter to his table in the Carriage Room coffee shop to take a call from a politician or his editor. Here reporters dined with important local politicians like Harry West, John Hume and Bill Craig. In the bar one met paramilitary leaders especially from the loyalist side, particularly the late Tommy Heron of the UDA. Journalists could be seen chatting at ease with men who had killed or who had ordered killings.

Deric Henderson, who worked for PA News, commented 'If only the walls of the Europa could speak. As listening posts go there was no place like it at the height of the Troubles in Northern Ireland. It was an international call centre and anybody in political life with message to deliver could be found on the premises. Notebooks and pens at the ready as the chain smoking Gerry Fitt held court in the Whip and Saddle. Or the thunderous Ian Paisley letting rip on the first floor'.

The foyer, Deric Henderson recalls, was the centre of activity within the hotel. 'It was here that the next day's stories were often dictated down a crackling telephone line to the copy takers in Fleet Street. Army, police, government officials, spooks and the men with highly questionable

backgrounds who once controlled loyalist paramilitary groups were regulars who gave freely with their time; just as long as the drinks were on you'. There is little wonder that Chris Ryder called it 'the crossroads of intrigue'.

Throughout those years of the 1970s all kinds of foreign accents could be heard as reporters from such diverse places as Brussels, Rome and New York broadcast home to their television views and radio listeners news of the trials and tribulations in Northern Ireland. The ITN reporter Gerald Seymour conceived the idea for his book *Harry's Game* whilst he was on duty in Northern Ireland.

Reporting The Troubles

Belfast in the 1970s was a war zone. The number of journalists who reported eyewitness accounts of troubled life in Northern Ireland without ever leaving the hotel is the stuff of much folklore. One report of riots in Belfast is reputed to have started with 'As I look over smoke-filled Belfast from my Europa hotel bedroom window…'. For the majority who took their jobs seriously, as the security situation worsened, staying and working in the Europa was not without its dangers. Simon Hoggart recalls:

"One hot summer Saturday afternoon a bunch of us were watching an international football match in my colour television when we heard an almighty gun battle going on in Turf Lodge. Two of us leapt out and drove up there, but when we arrived it was too dangerous to be outside. A widow took us in and we sheltered for two hours playing board games with her son. Then we left to go back to the Europa and we ran straight into an IRA roadblock and I remembered I had left my press card back at the hotel. IRA people tended to think that you were an army spy unless proved otherwise, so I expected 24 hours in a cellar somewhere. But my colleague was from *The Sun*, which was not then available in Northern Ireland. The IRA men

wanted to know why this was, when it had the best racing tipster in the business. Brian, my colleague, told them the glad tidings that it would be available from he autumn, and they waved us cheerily on our way. The large Bushmills I had in the upstairs bar of the Europa that night might have been the best drink I ever had during my stint."

Renagh Holohan, from *The Irish Times*, remembers having lunch in the dining room when a waiter ran through urging diners not to panic. "It was time to leave as the hotel was being evacuated. A bomb warning had been received and we gathered on the street outside. Glengall Street was cordoned off by the British Army. My little red Fiat was parked practically outside the Unionist Party Headquarters and I could see it from the military cordon. The bomb the soldier said was in the hotel car park. Could I get my car out? Yes, if I was quick, he said. I took a few footsteps forward and the bomb went off".

This is what she wrote in *The Irish Times* the next day. 'There was a huge bang which seemed to shake the ground and buildings for some time. I was knocked off my feet and fell into Great Victoria Street. Showers of glass and debris rained down and, looking up, I saw whole panes of glass fall from the Europa Hotel into Glengall Street. I got up and pulled my scarf down over my face and staggered across Great Victoria Street. I wandered around in the dust and debris for a while. People were screaming and running

in all directions. The smoke was so dense that it was hard to know what was going on. The ambulances arrived. People were taken off for treatment. I had no cuts or bruises, a trouser suit had seen to that, so I declined to go with them. But I was in a state of shock. I was probably closer to it than anyone else since I had got inside the cordon. I was lucky to get off so lightly'.

It was another bomb that brought her even closer to the Europa. 'In 1973 a huge car bomb, 150lb, went off directly outside the offices of *The Irish Times*. The five of us on the premises had to run past it when we got the army warning which was shouted up from the street. It destroyed all the buildings including our offices. So for a couple of months during the summer of 1973, *The Irish Times* moved into the Europa Hotel'.

Simon Hoggart's memories of Bloody Friday are particularly strong. He remembers, 'The whole of Belfast was in shock because of the wave of IRA bombs which killed many people. I was in the downstairs coffee bar when cooks and waitresses came rushing out and screaming that there was a bomb in the kitchens. We rushed into the lobby and I found that people had jammed the revolving door in the middle. So I went calmly down the line of swing doors to either side, turning locks while shouting "Don't panic, Don't panic". People hurled themselves at the swing doors, only to discover that in my cool way I had accidentally locked them rather than unlocked them. Luckily there was no bomb in the kitchen'.

In his book *Give Me Ten Seconds*, John Sergeant refers frequently to the Europa. He recalls a soldier walking up and down the road outside the hotel. He asked him what he was doing and was told that he thought there was a bomb in the vicinity. So Sergeant walked with him sharing solidarity. After a while they parted company and Sergeant went back to the Europa. The soldier walked on. Just a few seconds later there was a huge explosion and it turned out

to be Northern Ireland's first letter box bomb. It had gone off exactly where he had been talking to the soldier. It took him several hours just to realise how close they had both been to being killed – and the irony was that it didn't even make the news that night as there were subsequently larger bombs that day and no-one had been killed. Sergeant also recalls that he learnt many things about

Sir Max Hastings

the actual construction of bombs and was relieved to discover that the Europa was so strong that a bomb could never have brought the hotel down.

On occasion the threat of violence from outside the hotel would follow inside. Kate Adie talks in her autobiography, *The Kindness of Strangers*, about her time spent in Northern Ireland and at the Europa Hotel. She writes:

'Northern Ireland taught me one of the simpler aspects of fear: that threats used in your own language are far more frightening than anything delivered in a foreign language by people who look different. Surreal moments occur in Zaïrean police stations and Arab back alleys, when journalists look at each other and say "That finger across the throat stuff – do they really mean it?"

"Er maybe but they're jabbering away and it might just be their way of asking for quiet".

Going to your bedroom in the Europa Hotel in Belfast, having just got off a plane from London, to find the phone ringing and a voice saying "We know you're here" is a different matter, and it took me a couple of visits before I'd reply tartly "That's good, now how about a bit of room service with yourself minced up on a plate", before banging down the receiver and heading quickly for the bar'.

Death threats to journalists were common. Once a journalist had gone back on his word and reported something one of the Loyalist Paramilitaries had told him. The result was that anyone who worked for his particular paper had a death threat. A car park attendant was overheard by Simon Hoggart saying 'well, ye had better not go up the Shankill for a while, some of the fellas up there might be tempted to take a pop at ye. Now I think there is a space down there next to that Capri…' "They delivered very courteous death threats" notes Hoggart.

Derek Brown, who was *The Guardian*'s Northern Ireland correspondent from 1971 until 1977, started off staying at the Royal Avenue at £4 per night before being moved to the Europa at £6.50 per night. Whilst there he became the proud owner of a certificate congratulating him on surviving the Europa's 29th bomb!

Speaking of his time in the Europa, Simon Hoggart remembers that 'one time a bomb went off in the bus station behind the hotel while a *Sun* photographer was standing at the window. He was badly cut by flying glass. As his colleagues took him down in the lift, it stopped and Robert Fisk got in. As the victim sat on the floor, groaning, blood pouring from his head Fisk said "at least we've got our intro [first paragraph of a news story] for today. I gather they nearly hit him!"

A home from home

As in war zones throughout the world vicious violence was interspersed with boredom as journalists waited for something to happen. Those who stayed during these difficult days in Belfast remember the hotel with warmth and affection. Renagh Holohan, of *The Irish Times*, points out the uniqueness of the Europa back in the 1970s. 'When the Europa opened it provided an outlet new to Belfast. It had glamour and sophistication, however provincial, and Belfast was certainly provincial. It had soft lighting, a night club on the top floor where you could see all over the city from the mountains to the sea, and its location, size, complement of foreign staff and ability to provide some anonymity made it a natural base not just for visiting hacks but for local ones as well. There were a couple of good restaurants, loads of phones in the days when mobiles didn't exist and several bars and lounges.

'In the early days the large dining room was on the first floor, or was it the second? 'The Beefeater' was the place to go for dinner and the roast beef trolley was the thing to have. It was the trendiest place in the city. The Europa played host to press conferences and parties and every visitor, journalist or politician had to stay there if they were to keep up with events. The hotel was relatively safe thanks to the security checks at the gates. Those of us who lived in Belfast loved going there, even when we knew the menu by heart. Even had County Down the proliferation of gourmet restaurants it has now, it would not have been possible to leave the city. Communications were too bad – you couldn't even phone Dublin without going through the operator – so it was far too risky to leave Belfast on any other night other, for those of us on daily newspapers, than on Saturday'.

She continues, 'we recognised the smell of dead bodies at bomb sites, we covered harrowing stories, we were all CS gassed on various occasions, we had run before water cannons and rubber bullets, we knew the fear of being caught up in a riot or, worse, on the wrong side of one and we had all been involved in bomb alerts and even armed hold-ups. We knew the dread of missing a story and the endless tedium of the see-saw politics of the North. We lived hard and we played hard.

Trevor (now Sir Trevor) McDonald remembered the ten years he spent in Belfast reporting the Troubles for ITN.

Everyone knew the journalists were at the Europa and that they could be found there. 'It was the only place to be. It was a womb, an oasis, a home from home. There was even calm within the hotel'.

Sir Max Hastings; who covered Northern Ireland for the Daily Telegraph and the BBC at the time, and who went on to edit the Daily Telegraph and the London Evening Standard recalls:

'The Europa was a haven of tranquillity and comfort in the midst of mayhem for everybody who was lucky to stay there in the 1970s. One got used to losing a certain amount of glass in the windows when the bombs went off and to seeing all manner of crooks, thugs and even paid up killers in the restaurant among the journalists. Fully to savour the joys of the Europa, one needed to have stayed in the old Grand Central of Royal Avenue Hotel in the late 1960s. They were so awful that one used to welcome the riots to have an excuse to get out of them. People are always surprised to be told how much many of us enjoyed reporting from Northern Ireland 30 years ago when we were young, foolish and adventurous. Looking back, being able to retire to the Europa after a long day amid the flying rocks and bottles – and increasingly bullets – was one of the things that made it bearable'.

Simon Hoggart also describes the Europa as a 'very soothing place to work. You had to work around the clock, or at least be on duty at all hours of the day and night, so you didn't want to be bothered with cooking, cleaning of making your bed. I had a record player and arranged to have the only colour TV in the hotel in the room (they were still a luxury then). I had one of the single rooms at the back because you couldn't get the colour signal in the double rooms at the front. Sometimes I used to build model aeroplanes from kits, because it was utterly mindless and relaxing'.

At times Harper Brown appeared less than happy about having the hotel filled with 'riff-raff' from the press, Simon Hoggart recalls. 'A couple of us once complained about the slapdash service in the restaurant. He didn't seem surprised or concerned. "You see, they know you're getting it on your expense account" he said, as if that made it all right. Some nights a band played and Harper's idea of bliss was to see an elegantly dressed couple, the man perhaps in black tie, dancing gracefully on the small wooden dance floor. That was what the Europa was about, not hacks bellowing into the phones and getting drunk'.

Harper Brown often ran semi-formal dinner dances on Saturday evenings to which he usually invited Sir William Christie, a one-time Belfast Lord Mayor. He was the owner of Christie's wallpaper shops whose slogan was "We've got Belfast covered". It was not only Belfast's great and good that added a spot of glamour. Sir Max Hastings, then working for BBC Panorama, arrived one Sunday night in the lobby festooned with grouse. He had been shooting with Lord Larne and this was his share of the day's bag. Next day he told Simon Hoggart that he had asked the hotel kitchens to make the grouse the centrepiece of a dinner party. "It will be a very sophisticated affair – but you can come if you like", he told Hoggart. In the end the only other guests were Max's crew. One of them asked Hoggart what grouse tasted like. "Like chicken that's beginning to go off" he said. "I couldn't have put it better myself" said Max. The crew man said in that case, could he have steak? All the others had steak too and so Hastings and Hoggart worked their way through four roast birds'.

The upstairs bar was more often used in the evening, remembers Simon Hoggart, and was the scene of late drinking sessions at the end of the day. 'If you were feeling lavish, you could entertain in the restaurant where the speciality was Royal Barge Feasts – which we thought was a huge joke. Belfast being behind London, wine prices could be much lower than market price. Chateau La Tour could be had for £5, which seemed a lot then, but was roughly one fifth the London price". John Sergeant recalls that he often chose the wine as they all sat together. One occasion he asked Simon Winchester from *The Guardian* to chose the wine, which he proceeded to do – by the number. A surprised waiter produced a very old bottle of claret. It turned out to be £50 - a hugely expensive bottle of wine that the BBC's expenses would not run to. Embarrassed as they were, the wine was returned.

A special kind of air mail

Staying in the Europa was not without its lighter moments. There was much black humour attached to the frequency of the bomb attacks on the hotel, which soon had the nickname 'Hotel Eurupta'. On hearing that yet another device had been planted in the hotel foyer, one of the London-based journalists rushed to the reception desk to ask where the bomb had been planted. The battle-weary young

The Europa's temporary security hut in the early 1980s

woman pointed to the floor in the front desk where a large box had been left with the word 'bomb' written on it. This was another example of so called IRA humour. The journalists and the receptionist simply got on with their respective jobs as they waited for the Army bomb disposal team to arrive and locate the real device.

On another occasion the hotel had been evacuated because of a bomb scare. An American correspondent went up to Tommy Dunne, the head porter, and said he needed to see his pigeonhole because he was expecting an urgent letter. "Don't worry sir" said Tommy, "any minute now you'll be getting it by air mail".

When the late, and much loved, humorist Willy Rushton was asked by a young receptionist the straightforward question "Where did you hear about us?" she thought he would quote from one of the hotel's promotional brochures or a magazine article. His reply, however, was certainly not what she expected. Grinning from beneath his trademark beard Mr Rushton merely replied 'Oh, my dear, News at Ten'.

There was, not surprisingly, a strong camaraderie and sense of fun among the journalists who stayed. In quieter times the resident journalists indulged in practical jokes to pass the time and reduce the periods of boredom. A favourite joke was to have the restaurant telephone brought to the table by a waiter, ring the hotel and ask to speak to a new arrival plainly in view across the room. The hapless colleague was sent scurrying out the front door by the mysterious caller and across the road to meet the fictitious 'hooded defender' who 'had a great story to tell'. Other tricks included ordering an early breakfast for a newcomer who had overindulged the night before – many a hangover woke up to the enticing kippers, hot chocolate and *The Sun*!

The night reporter on the *News Letter* had the job of fetching the night news editor's fish and chips every night. One night he got fed up with doing this, so on his way he popped into the upstairs bar of the Europa for a convivial drink with the lads. After a while, he realised that his boss would be missing his supper, so he phoned in to say that he'd been passing the Markets area and had heard gunfire. He'd seen an army armoured car coming under fire from snipers. The night news editor rang the army in Lisburn, where they had heard nothing about it. So an armoured car was sent into the area, and it came under fire. Luckily no one was hurt.

To Bob Chesshyre, Northern Ireland correspondent for *The Observer* from 1971 until 1974 and now with *The Daily Telegraph*, the Europa was the Fleet Street of Belfast. He recalls that John Graham from *The Financial Times* was a long term resident in the hotel in the early 1970s and was the doyen of all the journalists who was renowned for his well-informed analytical articles. Every Thursday night he hosted a small dinner party in the Europa restaurant and used to invite favoured journalists to join him. If you were invited, it was a great accolade.

It did not do, however, to take yourself too seriously. Chris Ryder, who worked for *The Sunday Times* during the years he stayed at the Europa, 1971 until 1985, recalls once that a rather pompous journalist got the reply he deserved when asking what the prawns were like that day. The young waitress simply replied 'They're wee pink fish sir!'. The same man later asked what was on the wine list, to which came the response 'white, red and pink, sir!'. He recalls two country conference delegates of the SDLP coming down the circular staircase of the hotel. One was running his hands down the walls saying to a friend, 'Some place this is, they even have carpets on the walls'.

One group which benefited from the presence of so many young and naïve reporters were the taxi drivers who were always needed to take these men and women around the city to follow up the latest incident. These taxi men were totally fearless for they realised that they were sitting on a veritable goldmine. They knew that they would be handsomely paid for their work and, with their cabs on permanent standby at the hotel, they soon became part of the hotel staff. One inventive driver even carried with him sets of casual clothes so that the innocent newspaper men could change into them from their ridiculous suits and ties when they entered the less salubrious parts of Belfast. His foresight was much appreciated as the disguises may have saved the lives of more than a few journalists who regularly found themselves in totally alien situations.

Bigger than the moon landings

Many of the young reporters based in the Europa in those early days have since gone on to more illustrious careers. Gerald Seymour, then with ITN, became a very successful thriller writer. Simon Winchester of *The Guardian* is now a best selling author. Robert Fisk – who always stayed in room 707 – cut his teeth as a reporter for *The Times* and is now a high profile correspondent in the Middle East. Sir Max Hastings, then *The Daily Telegraph*'s man in Belfast, went on to edit two national newspapers after the Falklands War. John Sergeant, formerly ITN's political editor, is also a successful writer and major television and radio personality.

Among other journalists who are now household names and who were in the Europa early in their careers covering what was then the biggest running news story in Europe were Andrew Neil, now editor of *The Scotsman*, Bob Friend, now with Sky, and Terry Lloyd who died while reporting on the 2003 war in Iraq for ITN. Other noted journalists including Kate Adie, John Humphreys, Jeremy Paxman, Nick Witchell, Martyn Lewis, Anne Robinson, all now with the BBC, Trevor McDonald (who always bought a drink for the resident hotel pianist) and Colin Baker, then the United Press International reporter and now with ITN also stayed at the Europa. Simon Hoggart of *The Guardian* recalls that Belfast often received more news coverage than other significant events of the time such as the Munich Olympics and even moon landings.

An Established Europa

Circuit of Ireland Rally starts from the Europa

Spencer, Boots, Pennys and Dunnes to set up in Belfast. Investment in urban 'Making Belfast Work' schemes led to the reopening of the Grand Opera House, the development of Great Victoria Street and the emergence of the regeneration of Laganside. The two most high profile speculative ventures, however, did lead to much negative publicity. When successive Labour governments set up the De Lorean Motor Company at Dunmurry and the Learfan jet aircraft operation at Newtownabbey, they hoped that these firms would increase stability and employment in areas of greatest need and would be a positive way of countering community violence. Both firms were launched in a blaze of publicity yet, soon afterwards, both crashed equally publicly.

By the early 1980s life was beginning to return to some sense of normality and hotels regrouped and reorganised to ensure that they stayed open. If there were not going to be sufficient visitors to fill their rooms, then they would diversify and attract young people at the weekends to their discos and businessmen to their conference facilities. Discos took place in the luxurious surroundings of the fine dance floors and the conferences in the areas previously used for

Successive British governments made valiant efforts to kick-start new industries at a time when many, such as Rolls Royce, Albion, Peter Pan Bakeries and

Grundig, were scaling down their operations or closing down. Other long established firms, like Gallaher, Harland and Wolff, Sirocco Works, Goblin and

Mackies, were also shedding significant numbers of workers. The economic decline in the manufacturing industries was turning into a major crisis and, by 1981, 100

substantial operations in Northern Ireland had closed down.

There were, however, success stories too. The service industry sector was boosted following announcements by Marks and

Rally Launch

Guests looking out from the top floor windows could see clear evidence of the orgies of violence crippling Belfast. They witnessed tracer bullets and

had time to fill.
The Europa Hotel was an attractive target. It was a symbol of Government policy of bringing new life to Belfast and was easily accessible, situated right in the heart of the city. The bomb

Chapter 4

An Established Europa

A Shaky Northern Ireland Economy

Successive British governments made valiant efforts to kick-start new industries at a time when many, such as Rolls Royce, Albion, Peter Pan Bakeries and Grundig, were scaling down their operations or closing down. Other long established firms, like Gallaher, Harland and Wolff, Sirocco Works, Goblin and Mackies, were also shedding significant numbers of workers. The economic decline in the manufacturing industries was turning into a major crisis and, by 1981, 100 substantial operations in Northern Ireland had closed down.

There were, however, success stories too. The service industry sector was boosted following announcements by Marks and Spencer, Boots, Pennys and Dunnes to set up in Belfast. Investment in urban 'Making Belfast Work' schemes led to the reopening of the Grand Opera House, the development of Great Victoria Street and the emergence of the regeneration of Laganside. The two most high profile speculative ventures, however, did lead to much negative publicity. When successive Labour governments set up the De Lorean Motor Company at Dunmurry and the Learfan jet aircraft operation at Newtownabbey, they hoped that these firms would increase stability and employment in areas of greatest need and would be a positive way of countering community violence. Both firms were launched in a blaze of publicity yet, soon afterwards, both crashed equally publicly.

By the early 1980s life was beginning to return to some sense of normality and hotels regrouped and reorganised to ensure that they stayed open. If there were not going to be sufficient visitors to fill their rooms, then they would diversify and attract young people at the weekends to their discos and businessmen to their conference facilities. Discos took place in the luxurious surroundings of the fine dance floors and the conferences in the areas previously used for bedrooms and dining accommodation. By making these necessary changes the hotels could remain in business. Discos, conferences and weddings became the salvation of the hotel trade and the Europa was a forerunner in this innovation.

The Europa's Tenth Birthday

In July 1981 the Belfast Europa celebrated its 10th anniversary. In the decade since its opening, it had suffered many depredations. The repair bills had far exceeded the original £2 million cost of the hotel in 1971! However life was slightly better for the citizens of Belfast and Northern Ireland and the Europa management was determined to enjoy its birthday. The principal attraction on the day for the customers was the fact that all food and drink were to cost what the prices had been ten years earlier. That meant that a pint of beer would cost 32p and a measure of spirits just 33p, both less than half the 1981 prices. Even better value was to be found in the Carriage Room where a three course meal, consisting of soup, sirloin steak, a sweet and a pot of tea, would cost the princely sum of £2.02. Little wonder that the hotel did a roaring trade that day! Whilst the whole city was suffering a great deal during the past decade, the shopkeepers and businessmen and women had looked up to the Europa for a lead in the darkest days and looked forward to the next ten years with a degree of optimism.

The hotel foyer in 1983

And there was good news at the end of the financial year which ended in September 1981. The Europa was, at last, making a profit. The hotel was out of the red and was holding its head above water. A greater degree of normality in Belfast city centre was the chief reason for the upturn in fortune. The welcome reduction in violence was encouraging local businessmen to begin to use the hotel as a conference venue once more. Hard-headed entrepreneurs were prepared to book into the Europa and business began to flourish again. During the week the hotel was regularly fully booked with receptions and conferences making use of the facilities which it had to offer. At weekends there still were empty beds and accommodation but, with lots of positive advertising, tourists were returning to Belfast and choosing to stay at the Europa. Harper Brown was even arranging special weekend package deals to attract fishermen to come on trips to Northern Ireland's magnificent angling loughs, using the Europa as their accommodation base. The strategy was beginning to have some success.

Another element which played into the hands of the Europa was the reopening, after a year and following further bomb damage, of the Grand Opera House, located practically next door to the hotel. Designed by Frank Matcham in the style of the London West End theatres, the Grand Opera House has been described as one of the finest regional theatres outside London. Naturally enough the hotel was being chosen by the stars

Harper Brown with the winner of a Miss Forum contest

of the various shows who were performing at the Opera House. The Belfast public had been starved of decent entertainment and they were soon flocking back to enjoy the spectacular shows and plays which were on stage.

Tourist brochures were again marketing the Europa Hotel as a premier spot to stay in Northern Ireland and, in conjunction with the hotel's own public relations staff, this aggressive campaigning was having a great deal of success. The buzz seemed to be back in Belfast and the Europa was benefiting from the new feeling of confidence and prosperity.

Change of Name – the Forum Hotel

On 1 February 1983 the people of Belfast, passing along Great Victoria Street to their places of work, looked up at the Europa as they did every day – and stopped in their tracks. The name outside the hotel had been changed and, instead of their much loved Europa, they saw a new, and altogether more uncomfortable, name - 'Forum'. It so happened that Grand Metropolitan Hotels Limited had become Grand Metropolitan Trading and part of their group was called Forum Hotels International. 'Branding' was, at that time, the new management fad. By 1983, this part of the trading group owned the Europa. They had no intention of retaining the Europa name and decided to change it. It may have become the Forum from that February day onwards but it was still the dear old Europa to the locals. Even taxi drivers would make mistakes and take clients to the Antrim Forum leisure centre twenty miles away instead of to the city centre hotel!

The best story, however, about the renaming of the hotel was related by an English travel agent. A gentleman had to come across to Belfast to visit Northern Ireland Electricity staff and asked the travel agent to book him into a Belfast hotel, but definitely not the Europa! So the travel agent duly booked him into

The Forum Hotel, sporting its new logo (top left)

Staff celebrate the hotel's 12th birthday

the Forum Hotel. On the way back to the airport the man told the taxi driver how much he had enjoyed his stay in Belfast and how helpful and friendly everyone had been. Belfast, he said, was not the terrible city it was made out to be on the news. The taxi driver asked the man where he had stayed and he was told the story of how he had asked to be accommodated anywhere but the Europa. Imagine the dismay of the businessman when the taxi driver told him he had been in the Europa all the time and that its name had just been changed earlier in the year! And so it was that, although the name on the building was now Forum, everybody continued to speak of the Europa.

Harper Brown's Retirement and Death

From the beginning of the 1980s, Harper Brown had been ill. He had exhausted himself in his dedication to the needs of the Europa and had to spend time recovering in the Mayfair and Fleming's hotels in London. He suffered from emphysema and, in January 1985, he decided to retire on the grounds of ill health. His employers, Grand Metropolitan, expressed deep regret that Harper was leaving. He had led his team in the most trying circumstances possible; he had laboured under extreme pressure. They wished him well for his retirement. But it was the customers and staff who were going to miss Harper most of all. He, himself, found the wrench from the place that had been his life the most difficult of all. Late in 1986, he was greatly honoured when the former 'Whip and Saddle Bar' was named after him. It became 'Harper's Bar', a name which was to remain for many years to come.

Sadly, on Boxing Day 1989, Harper Brown died at his home off the Upper Malone Road in south Belfast. He was just 61 years old. Probably the greatest tribute was paid to him by John Miskimmin, for years the general manager at the Slieve Donard Hotel in Newcastle and a friend with whom he had shared an Ulster Transport Authority training. He praised Harper as having been 'quite simply the best hotel manager I have met in my life'. Lord Mayors and VIPs paid tribute to a man whom they had appreciated and greatly loved. Billy Hastings added his words of respect describing Harper as 'an extremely talented manager'.

Under New Management

John O'Carroll took over when Harper Brown retired early in 1985 and was general manager until 1986. He had worked for Intercontinental when they were bought over by Grand Metropolitan who immediately rationalised their holdings across the United Kingdom and sold off their hotels, except the Belfast Europa. This was when it was the Forum Hotel.

These years were more positive for Northern Ireland and he was in charge of the hotel when the political situation was more normal and journalists were coming over, not to cover riots, but rather to report on the progress of the peace talks. Things were looking up in Belfast with the Grand Opera House in full swing and the Europa beds in great demand. John admitted that the standards in the hotel were not superlative but there were few other hotels in the area except their main opposition - the Wellington Park Hotel. Staff were content and turnover was low. He was always impressed by the sense of goodwill amongst the population and the fact that the local people supported the hotel in the good times and the bad.

Further Changes

Staff were soon to face another major change. In October 1986 the hotel was sold, in double quick time, to Colin Noble and some of his directors who had apparently just walked uninvited into the Intercontinental Hotel in London and asked to buy the Belfast Europa. Their Emerald Group already owned the Travel Lodge in the Canadian city of Winnipeg and two hotels in Londonderry and one in County Donegal. Belfast-born Colin Noble, the founder of this hotel group, had formed the company in 1981 at the time of his purchase of his first hotel in Winnipeg. The vendors of that hotel, so the story goes, said to Noble 'I suppose your company's called Emerald Hotels', whereupon he looked sheepishly at his colleagues and said 'Oh, yes, that's absolutely right!' The staff at the Forum Hotel prepared themselves for their new owners

Colin Noble, Mima Harper and Peter French, directors of Emerald Hotels, restoring the Europa's original name

Emerald Hotels

The first thing that Colin Noble did was to change the name of the hotel back to the Europa. It was a popular decision. From the beginning, the new management style was one of keeping a low profile. The purchase of the hotel by Emerald had taken most pundits by surprise. There had been only the briefest of mentions of the sale in the Belfast press and the subject of the amount paid for the prestigious city centre site remained secret. Peter French was determined to get on quietly and efficiently with turning the failing fortunes of the Europa around. He was well qualified for the job.

Born in England and married to a Northern Irish wife, French possessed an impressive pedigree in hotel management. He had worked in a number of high class hotels in London and New York before becoming the youngest ever resident manager at the exclusive Mandarin Oriental Hotel in Hong Kong. There he had upgraded the hotel and had won for it the ultimate prize by being voted the Best Hotel in the World in 1984 and 1985. As a result, French had himself been accorded the accolade of Manager of the Year in 1985. In 1986 he had joined the Emerald Group with a view to coming to the Belfast Europa as its local supremo.

and their dynamic managing director and general manager, Peter French, with inevitable feelings of apprehension. What lay in store for them under the new regime?

He was determined to upgrade the entire operation. In fact the first thing he had to do was to give the hotel a thorough cleaning. The years of persistent damage had allowed parts of the building to fall into what the directors described as a 'dreadful state'. One of their first tasks was to renovate the restaurant and present the menus with a more international flavour. A new pastry kitchen and a revitalised coffee shop gave the old 'Carriage Room' a breath of fresh air. The bedroom accommodation, too, was completely refurbished at the cost of £1.7 million and visitors were now being offered what was being advertised as 'unrivalled luxury'. Changes were also made to the staff structure to inject new blood into the organisation.

Another of the key figures in the Emerald empire was the talented Mima Harper. She had vast experience in the hotel trade and had been an original director of the company with Colin Noble since it started trading in 1981 with the purchase of their hotel in Winnipeg. She managed that hotel until 1987 and had, since the purchase of the Europa, regularly commuted from Canada to Belfast to attend board meetings. In 1987 she came to Belfast to manage the Europa but still spent one week each month, for a period of eighteen months, managing the Winnipeg hotel. This travelling commitment would have left most people tired and jaded, but to Mima it was all part of the job. She relished the opportunity to remain a vital cog in the wheel both in Canada and in Northern Ireland.

Emerald Convention Centre

David Boyce, resident manager from 1986 until 1991, had fond memories of the Europa in those Emerald days. He was successful in obtaining the accommodation business for all the guests of the Kelly Show, a popular chat show on Ulster Television. The Europa, he remembered, was the only hotel in the British Isles running at 30% full rate bookings when a room cost £93 per night. Often the hotel was completely full during mid-week. Had the management resisted the temptation of buying the Lancaster Gate Hotel in London, then, according to David, the Europa, and the Emerald Group, would have gone from strength to strength.

Refurbishing the Hotel

The principal changes at the Europa were concentrated on improving the conference facilities and the expansion of the banqueting arrangements. The Emerald directors saw the future of the hotel in attracting commercial interests during the day and concentrating on social events in the evening. A central location was ideal for these purposes and Colin Noble and Peter French were determined to cash in on its every advantage. By October 1989, the Europa's excellent Emerald Convention Centre was in full operation. It was capable of seating 1,000 conference delegates on revolutionary Shelby Williams Action chairs whilst their feet rested upon the finest Irish spun carpets. The centre, created at a cost of £4 million, was the most impressive in Ireland with eight £50,000 chandeliers hanging from its ceiling and a surround of cherry wood walls specially imported from Canada. These superb features still enhance the Europa's grand ballroom to this day. This top class accommodation was certain to secure Belfast's place on the international conference circuit, with the hotel's professional event-organising team putting the pleasure back into setting up such major events.

Emerald Hotels were confident that, through their sponsorship of such events as the Ulster Hardcourt Tennis Championships, business could be won from far and wide. The hotel was the venue for a most noteworthy Institute of Directors' Cross Border Trade Conference which was addressed by the then Irish Taoiseach, Charles Haughey. At the time Ireland held the Presidency of the European Union and Mr Haughey was, consequently, its President. Understandably the visit to Northern Ireland by such a 'hate figure' to Unionists as Charles Haughey drew much vehement criticism from many in this section of the community. For a time it seemed that the conference would have to be cancelled because of the public furore, but, in the end, and with stalwart assistance from the police, the event was celebrated as a great success.

Another large and important international conference held in the centre in August 1990 was a three day meeting to discuss the topic – 'Ireland, the way Forward'. Over 400

delegates attended from all parts of the world, including the United States, Canada, Australia and Europe.

In 1990 it was decided to close the Penthouse, dispense with the Poppets and move in a different direction. Later that year the new night-club, 'Paradise Lost', became a popular

Two photographs of staff and onlookers taken at the Rothman's Circuit of Ireland Rally in 1987 - an event which started from the Europa for several years during the 1980s

venue for the city's young people and it remained a busy and successful nightspot for years to come. When it opened, after much publicity which attracted many high profile guests and celebrities, it was regularly patronised by the city's young and affluent night club set. It was a self-contained unit with a separate entrance in Glengall Street at the side of the hotel which did not affect the smooth running of the Europa itself.

Emerald Hotels were determined to attract visitors to their Irish hotels which included, apart from the Europa in Belfast, the Everglades and White Horse in Londonderry and the Redcastle in Moville in County Donegal. Their motto was 'Join the Emerald Set – it's created for you'. Whilst the Everglades and the White Horse were recording only a small profit at the time, the Europa – the 'cash cow' of the Group – was a highly profitable business with operating profits in excess of £1 million.

Trouble Ahead

The changes which had been effected at the Europa since its purchase by Emerald Hotels brought much needed additional prosperity to the centre of Belfast, and visitors and conference delegates were enjoying the hotel's facilities. Money had been spent and more had been committed to ensure the Europa's prominent place in the entertainment and commercial world. By the late 1980s and the early 1990s, the underlying threat of world recession was growing. At the end of 1990, Emerald's main bank, the Alliance and Leicester Building Society, was becoming decidedly anxious. It had loaned £23 million to Emerald to assist expansion plans and, on examination of the Group's accounts, saw clearly the weaknesses within its management structure, although they were aware that trading at the Europa itself was buoyant. High interest rates and the effects of the recent

Gulf War were also proving insurmountable.

Although it was true that Emerald had bought the Europa at an advantageous price from Grand Metropolitan, the directors now realised that they were seriously overspent and were running out of cash. But it was the purchase, at the height of the property boom in London, of the privately owned 40 bedroom Lancaster Gate Hotel in the capital, for over £7 million, with its empty beds and urgent need to refurbish, that became the real millstone around Emerald's neck. In every likelihood the Europa might have

EUROPA HOTEL
BELFAST

Welcome

Great Victoria Street Belfast BT2 7AP N. Ireland
Tel: (0232) 327000   Telex: 74491 EUROPA

CASINO ROYALE

♠

NEW YEARS EVE PROGRAMME
Welcome Reception: 7.00 pm Bucks Fizz on arrival
First spin of Roulette Wheel: 7.00 – 8.00 pm
Dinner: 7.45 – 9.15 (last orders for dinner)
Music: 8.30 "JOHN ANDERSON BIG BAND"
Second spin of Roulette Wheel: 10.30 – 11.30 pm
"GERRY KELLY LIVE": 11.55 – 1.30 am
Midnight: Celebrate Happy New Year into New Years Day
Dance to: JOHN ANDERSON BIG BAND 1.30 – 2.00 am

CASINO ROYALE

♠

NEW YEAR'S DAY 1990
LUNCH TIME BUFFET LUNCH
£12.75

Children under 12 years £6.00
Children under 5 years Free
Casino will spin from 12.00 – 12.45 pm
Lunch: 12.00 – 1.30 pm
Casino will spin from 2.00 – 3.00 pm
Childrens entertainment will be provided after lunch.

For further information contact:
CASINO ROYALE BOOKING OFFICE
Europa Hotel
Great Victoria Street Belfast
Tel: (0232) 327000

Emerald Hotels

GERRY KELLY
LIVE AT THE
CASINO ROYALE
♠
NEW YEARS EVE 1989
EURÓPA HOTEL

A flyer from one of the themed New Year's Eve parties held at the Europa - the 1989-90 theme was 'Casino Royale' hosted by chat show presenter Gerry Kelly

been able to survive had it not been for the unequal burden of the London operation.

Following considerable debate, Mima Harper, alone of all the directors, recalled how strongly she had advised against the purchase of the Lancaster Gate. Considering that it was too expensive and would have taken a great deal of money to improve it, she felt that they could have walked away from the commitment to buy. Her colleagues, anxious to gain a foothold in London, out voted her and proceeded to buy the prestige hotel. given Mima's operational experience, she had to go to London to endeavour to revive the fortunes of the

Lancaster Gate. . As property prices fell and recession hit the UK economy, hers was an impossible mission and it was not long before the London hotel brought the company down.

Michael Williamson, who had joined the company as financial controller in 1990, was also wary of the proposed London purchase. He knew that the Europa was the only hotel in the Emerald Group which was achieving significant profits and advised that further expansion was premature. He argued that the focus should be on consolidation and rationalisation rather than growth for growth's sake and that all efforts should be made to concentrate on the Europa to maximise income. The weaker hotels, he considered, should be disposed of too. Appreciating the difficult economic problems of the late 1980s and early 1990s he expressed his reservations, although his advice was also set aside.

Emerald also owned a Bewley's franchise in Belfast and the Pizza Hut franchise in Northern Ireland, but such a diverse range of business activities led to financial difficulties. This led the Alliance and Leicester to take the decision to call in the receiver. The building society agreed to keep the Europa open as a going concern, which they considered would make the sale to prospective buyers more attractive. And so the saga, which Billy Hastings would later describe as 'the longest saga since Dallas', began. It would still be some time before the future of the Europa was to be secured.

The Receiver Arrives

On Monday 22 April 1991, the Emerald directors were set aside and the receiver came into the hotel to brief the staff and to hold a press conference for the trades unions and the local papers. Although everyone involved knew that changes were on the way, the arrival of Stephen Prenter, the receiver, came as a shock. It was not long before the Europa personnel got to know the new, albeit temporary, supremo and what they could expect from him and his firm. They were heartened to hear that the hotel would continue to trade and that the majority of the staff would be retained. Inevitably, in order to trim unnecessary costs, there were to be a number of redundancies but these would be dealt with in a fair and professional manner. Michael Williamson took over as general manager early in the summer of 1991. The chief objective for the receivers, however, was a pragmatic one - to act in the best interest of the creditors and of the building society.

Stephen Prenter and his Plans for the Future of the Europa

Stephen Prenter had two options for the Europa. He could, as is often the case in such circumstances, simply close down the hotel and liquidate the assets. On the other hand he could decide to trade on and then sell the hotel as a going concern at the most opportune time. Both the Alliance and Leicester Building Society and Stephen Prenter himself chose the latter option for a number of reasons, some political and the others financial. To have summarily shut down such a recognisable icon on the Belfast landscape would have sent out completely the wrong message to tourists and investors alike.

The hotel did, of course, have many other advantages. It was centrally located in the city; it was in reasonable structural order and, above all, it was actually making money. Stephen Prenter considered that the Europa would be the first of the Group's properties to be sold. Subsequent events were to prove otherwise. The then economy minister, Richard Needham, was also expressing encouragement and confidence in the future of the hotel

Stephen Prenter

industry, although he did note that there was an under-provision of hotel beds and hoped that major international chains would come to Northern Ireland. On a more human and practical note the actor, Howard Keel, who had been performing his swansong concert in the Grand Opera House, was one of many guests who, on hearing the news of the receivership, had expressed his relief that he still had a bed for the night!

Stephen Prenter wasted no time in advertising the hotel in British, Northern Irish and Republic of Ireland newspapers on 1 May 1991 offering for sale as a group or individually the three Emerald hotels, the Europa, the Everglades and the White Horse. The price for the Europa was reputed to be between £9 and £12 million and for the Londonderry hotels £2 and £1.75 million respectively. Two major hotel concerns from the Republic, including the Jury's Hotel Group, expressed interest. Within a few days, however, they had withdrawn. Hastings Hotels became one of the front runners amongst a number of other local businesses vying for ownership. It was the first of many offers that Billy Hastings made during the period of receivership.

Stephen Prenter had also engaged the interest of international hoteliers in talks to buy the Europa. He spent time in London and elsewhere with the Hilton, Hyatt, Marriott and Holiday Inn chains, amongst others, marketing the Europa. The Northern Ireland Tourist Board was also keen that an international 'brand' should buy the Europa as it was their belief that it would place Belfast firmly on the international tourist destination map. But, before the year was out, further disaster struck the hotel to jeopardise the best laid plans of the receiver.

The Christmas Bomb - 1991

On 4 December 1991, a 1,000lb bomb at the Europa added further to the management's woes. For some time life seemed relatively peaceful in Belfast and so this outrage came as a shock. In fact it had been over a decade since a bomb had affected the hotel and there were now very few staff who had any experience of dealing with this eventuality. At the hotel that evening a large Institute of Chartered Surveyors function was being held in the banqueting room. The banqueting manager, Philip Drennan, informed those attending that there had been a bomb warning phoned into the hotel and he requested them to leave.

Many of the diners, somehow hoping that the call was a hoax, dallied over their meal. Realising the danger, Philip then emphasised the urgency of quitting the premises without further ado and, to encourage his guests to leave the hotel immediately, he suggested that they took their wine glasses with them. They left the hotel reluctantly and

The aftermath of the IRA van bomb attack on the Europa, 20 May 1993

had then to be sent round to Blackstaff Square to ensure that they were in a safe area. Hundreds of black-tied professional gentlemen arrived in the square complete with wine bottles and wine glasses in their hands to be confronted with the resident frequenters of the square – a large number of black leather-clad bikers drinking bottles of Budweiser and Bass! There was little time for the two groups to become acquainted before a terrific explosion sent sheets of glass into Great Victoria Street.

One touching story of gallantry emerged from this distressing incident. As the gentlemen and their ladies were leaving the hotel to take up their positions in Blackstaff Square, a young lady, clearly in great distress and clothed only in a dressing gown, appeared amongst them. One of the black-tied guests, a civil engineer, approached her and offered her his coat to keep her warm. After thanking him for his kindness she blurted out that her clothes and car keys were still in her Europa bedroom. She had no idea what she was going to do. Thinking on his feet, the young man offered to take her to his home for the night and return her next day to retrieve her belongings, saying that he was sure his wife would be delighted that he had been able to be of assistance. Unfortunately for him it was late when he got home and his wife was already in bed. He had, therefore, been unable to explain the situation. He might, in hindsight, have been advised to have wakened his wife because when she got up next morning to find a young lady wearing a Europa bathrobe asleep on her sofa, he had a lot of explaining to do!

As it transpired, the expert bomb-disposal men had almost been able to defuse the bomb but for the fact that the IRA's strategy of giving reasonable warnings had changed. It was reputed that the terrorists had become alarmed that the Army bomb-disposal squads had become so proficient at defusing bombs that they had heartlessly decided to reduce the time given for warnings.

After an inspection the very next day, surveyors Kirk McClure Morton reported that the damage was extensive, with an estimated repair bill of around £3 million. Every window was broken; several bedrooms were severely damaged; pipes and cables were dislodged and the loading bay in Glengall Street had been destroyed. It was estimated

The Grand Opera House suffered extensive damage following a bomb which exploded in Glengall Street in December 1991

that the repairs would take seven months to complete. Despite the devastation, the hotel reopened five days later for the Publicity Association of Northern Ireland gala dinner. The

Joy Hastings with Hollywood star Howard Keel

glittering occasion proceeded with the guests entering the hotel through large and unsightly hardboard tunnels. The evening included an appearance by the local television celebrity, Gerry Kelly, who hosted his regular weekly show towards the end of the proceedings. But, despite the dogged spirit of everyone concerned, their gala celebration had to be abruptly concluded when a further bomb scare was phoned into the hotel. Everyone had to leave the premises as quickly as possible.

The hotel had remained open for business, as promised, since the date of receivership proceedings. The bomb in December 1991 radically changed the hotel's prospects and disrupted Christmas bookings to the tune of £1 million at the hotel's very busiest time of the year. A price tag of £10 million was being bandied about in the press, as well as the probability that this amount would be considerably reduced following the bomb damage.

The Europa remained in the hands of the receiver for two years. In the intervening period life carried on much as before with the hotel continuing to trade very profitably. It still continued to play host to many of the world's top entertainers – Paul Simon, Bob Dylan, Sir Cliff Richard and Sir Peter Ustinov to name but a few. Life went on although hotel staff had to deal with 250 bomb warnings between the Christmas 1991 bomb and the sale of the hotel in 1993.

It was not until the early months of 1993 that renewed speculation about the Hastings Hotels Group's continuing interest in the purchase of the Europa emerged. Billy Hastings had always wanted to have the Europa Hotel as part of his ever-increasing portfolio. Local Belfast newspaper reports of 13 May 1993 confirmed the Hastings Hotels interest but the receiver scuppered rumours that Billy Hastings was the only interested party. Stephen Prenter informed the Belfast community that there was, in fact, a hard core of eight parties who were showing an interest in purchasing the Europa.

The Hilton Group - whose representative visited on six occasions - and Holiday Inns were also backing a number of local consortia although it was fair to say that the international hotel groups were, if anything, a little less interested in the Europa now that the severe effects of the world recession were taking hold. However it was clear, despite the downturn in the economy, that the future of the Europa was being keenly fought over. Stephen Prenter expressed his total confidence that, at last, the hotel would soon be sold and was hopeful that his guide price of £10 million would be achieved. But just as this report and its ramifications were being taken in, there came another cruel blow to the receiver's plans.

The Bomb Calculated to Scupper the Sale

Shortly before 8 o'clock on the morning of Thursday 20 May 1993, the day when the local council election results were being counted, a hijacked skip lorry, parked close to the Grand Opera House, and containing between 500-1,000lb of explosives, was blown apart by a massive blast. Many buildings in the area were extensively damaged. One entire side of the Grand Opera House simply caved in. The Crown Bar, possibly Belfast's best known public house, was severely damaged. Ulster Unionist Headquarters in Glengall Street and the Ulsterbus depot close by were devastated. The main target was, of course, the Europa where a huge gaping hole had been smashed in the side wall, with shattered glass from every one of its windows being blown in every direction. The only positive aspect of this explosion was the fact that the new Great Northern Mall, situated right next door to the Europa, did not suffer any damage at all because of its totally bomb proof structure.

Stephen Prenter outside the damaged Europa Hotel, May 1993

Fortunately only a handful of people in the vicinity had been injured, thanks mainly to the speed of evacuation from the hotel and the surrounding areas. The cost of the repairs was likely to be enormous, with the resultant disruption to the commercial heart of Belfast difficult to measure. For the foreseeable future the hotel struggled on with a slight reduction in the numbers of staff. Inevitably some workers had to be laid off, but this was kept to a minimum.

For Stephen Prenter, the bomb was yet another severe headache. The sale was hanging in the balance. He had been close to finalising the sale of the Europa after two years of receivership. He now had to sharpen his focus by taking a tricky decision. He could sell the hotel at a much reduced price or he could have it repaired and adhere to his original £10 million asking price. He expected that the government would settle a fair compensation claim which would mean that the total price he could anticipate would still match his original valuation or be very close to it. All was not doom and gloom and, although prospective buyers, especially those from Great Britain or Europe, would be frightened off, there were still a number of local interested parties.

The front-runner was Billy Hastings. He was contacted by the press soon after the bomb had exploded and asked if he would still be keen to make the purchase. His cautious response was that he would have to wait and see what the cost of the damage was likely to be before he would decide whether to remain in the race or withdraw from it. A damaged Europa was better than no Europa, although his business sense kept him from making an immediate decision. The matter needed most serious consideration and, at the same time, Billy underwent a successful quadruple heart bypass operation followed by a lengthy recuperation.

Meanwhile repairs were being carried out on the hotel and, because of this, the number of rooms available for occupancy was reduced to just one third of its full complement of 200.

On 2 August 1993, the Europa Hotel was finally bought by the Hastings Hotels Group. The price, according to the local press, was around £7 million. The discussions in the days before the deal was clinched were extremely tense. Stephen Prenter remembers a number of meetings when Billy Hastings and he were just on the point of signing when another obstacle barred the way to a deal. Billy Hastings had a secret weapon when it came to finalising the matter of buying a great hotel: he wore his lucky green jacket. On the first couple of occasions it did not bring him success but eventually on 2 August one determined rub of that green cloth brought him his ultimate achievement. The Europa was his. He had bought the hotel for £4.4 million although he had greatly strained his finances in covering the costs of the purchase in order to achieve his goal. He had bought the bricks and mortar only in its damaged state and did not benefit from the Northern Ireland Office compensation which went to the receivers. And, at the same time, two of Billy's other properties, the Stormont and Fir Trees hotels, were badly damaged in further terrorist explosions. But, as an eternal optimist, he looked forward to transforming the image of the Belfast Europa.

Celebrity chef Ainsley Harriot with Billy Hastings

Celebrity Visitors

Above, Actor Elliot Gould with John Toner
Right, Singer Natalie Imbruglia with Paddy
Harbison

Left, Singer Tony Bennett with Carolyn Stalker, front office manager
Below, Local actor James Nesbit with Nicole McMahon

Above, Comedian Frank Carson with the Europa's concierge Kris Kavanagh
Right, Singer Darius with the Europa's Emma Johnston

Left, Representatives from BT Northern Ireland and the Carryduff Manchester United Supporters' Club with Sir Alex Ferguson Below, Alan Whicker with Europa's Valerie Bacalhau

Left, Billy Hastings with former Conservative Party Leader William Hague

Above, War correspondent Kate Adie with John Toner
Right, TV personality Des O'Connor with Carolyn Stalker

THE LOBBY BAR

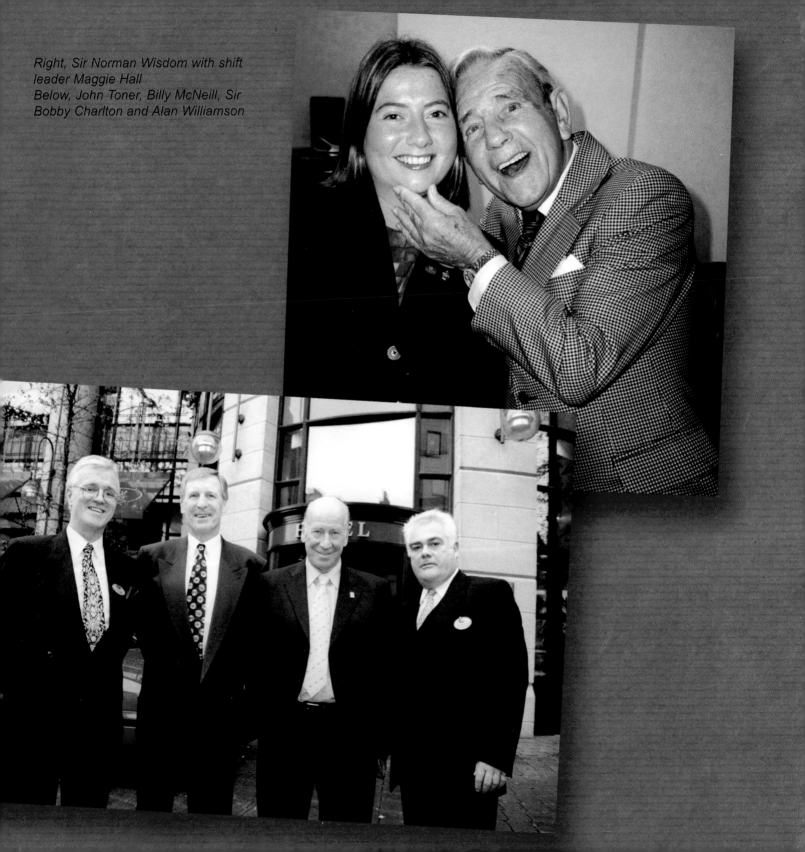

Right, Sir Norman Wisdom with shift leader Maggie Hall
Below, John Toner, Billy McNeill, Sir Bobby Charlton and Alan Williamson

THE LOBBY BAR →

Left, Katie Derham with head barman Paddy McAnerney
Below, Paul Daniels (centre) with staff members Thomas McKnight and Mohammed Abou Saleh

Right, Dennis Law and George Best with the Europa's Tom Cotter
Below Right, Archbishop Desmond Tutu with John Toner

WINE OF THE MONTH £16
WYNDHAM ESTATE CHARDONNAY

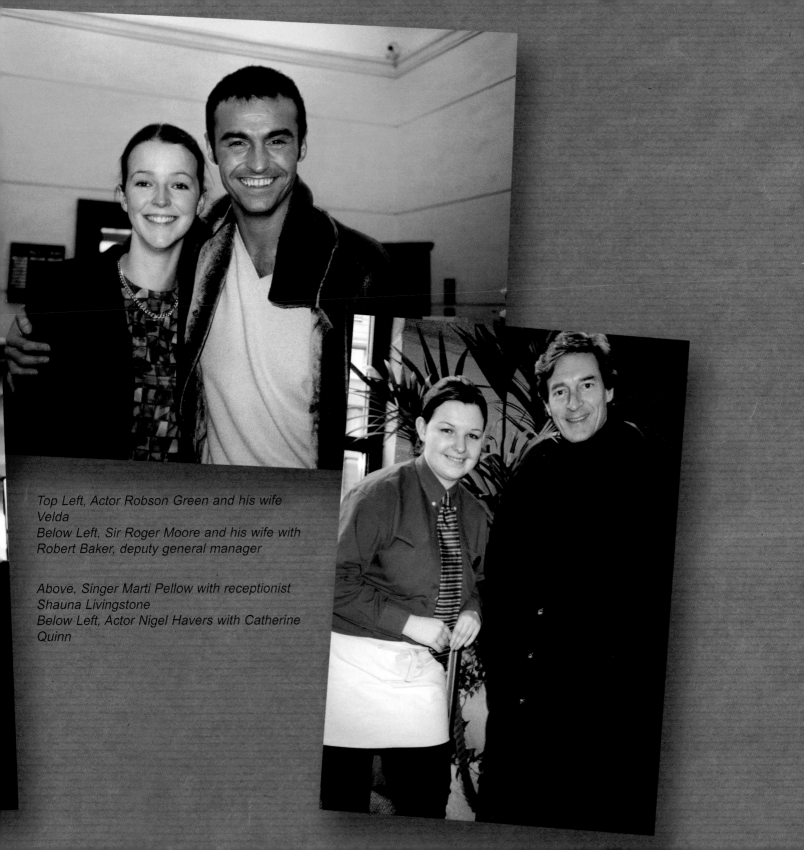

Top Left, Actor Robson Green and his wife Velda
Below Left, Sir Roger Moore and his wife with Robert Baker, deputy general manager

Above, Singer Marti Pellow with receptionist Shauna Livingstone
Below Left, Actor Nigel Havers with Catherine Quinn

*Left, Bianca Jagger signs the Europa's guest book
Below, Howard Hastings with former Secretary of State Mo Mowlam*

Below, Singer Paul Young with receptionist Donna Lineham

Above, Elaine Paige with Europa's head porter, Jimmy Connor. Right, Actress Patricia Hodge with concierge Brian Noade.

An American President Comes to Stay

By August 1993, therefore, the Europa Hotel was in the ownership of the Hastings Hotels Group. Since the bomb in the previous May the options for the receiver, Stephen Prenter, had been limited. Billy Hastings was the only man with the courage and the cash to buy the gutted shell of the Europa. Although he had the full support of his son Howard, the company's managing director, and Edward Carson, the financial director and vice chairman, Billy, by now almost fully recovered from a heart operation, ran into some problems.

The President steps off Airforce One at Belfast International Airport

He felt that his endeavours to buy the hotel were being thwarted by the Northern Ireland Tourist Board chiefs and by government ministers, including the Secretary of State, Sir Patrick Mayhew, who wished to attract a large hotel 'brand' name from Great Britain or elsewhere to locate in Belfast. Hugh O'Neill, the Tourist Board chairman, and

Richard Needham, the economy minister, seemed so focussed and determined on a 'brand' - much to the detriment of the local hoteliers, principal amongst them being Billy Hastings and

Hastings Hotels. They believed that to have a Hilton, a Hyatt, a Holiday Inn or a Marriott in Northern Ireland would have sent out a signal that it was no longer dangerous to visit Belfast.

But, in the end, none of these companies was keen to proceed and the way was left open for Billy to add the Europa to the Group. The price – just £4.4 million.

In October 1992, in his inaugural speech as president of the Chartered Institute of Marketing, Billy Hastings attacked government policies which concentrated investment on industries which

By August 1993, therefore, the Europa Hotel was in the ownership of the Hastings Hotels Group. Since the bomb in the previous May the options for the receiver, Stephen Prenter, was ... Billy Hastings was

buy the hotel were being thwarted by the Northern Ireland Tourist Board chiefs and by government ministers, including the Secretary of State, Sir Patrick Mayhew, who wished to attract a large hotel 'brand' name from Great Britain or elsewhere to ... in Belfast. Hugh O'Neill, ... and

sent out a signal that it was no longer dangerous to visit Belfast. But, in the end, none of these companies was keen to proceed and the way was left open for Billy to add the Europa to the Group. The price – just £4.4 million.

In October 1992, in his inaugural speech as president of the

Presidential Suite

Chapter 5

An American President Comes to Stay

By August 1993, therefore, the Europa Hotel was in the ownership of the Hastings Hotels Group. Since the previous May's bomb the options for the receiver, Stephen Prenter, had been limited. Billy Hastings was the only man with the courage and the cash to buy the gutted shell of the Europa. Although he had the full support of his son Howard, the company's managing director, and Edward Carson, the financial director and vice chairman, Billy, by now almost fully recovered from a heart operation, ran into some problems.

He felt that his endeavours to buy the hotel were being thwarted by the Northern Ireland Tourist Board chiefs and by government ministers, including the Secretary of State, Sir Patrick Mayhew, who wished to attract a large hotel 'brand' name from Great Britain or elsewhere to locate in Belfast. Hugh O'Neill, the Tourist Board chairman, and Richard Needham, the economy minister, seemed focussed and determined on a 'brand' – much to the detriment of the local hoteliers, principal amongst them being Billy Hastings and Hastings Hotels. They believed that to have a Hilton, a Hyatt, a Holiday Inn or a Marriott in Northern Ireland would send out a signal that it was no longer dangerous to visit Belfast. In the end, none of these companies was keen to proceed and the way was left open for Billy to add the Europa to the Group. The price – just £4.4 million.

In October 1992, in his inaugural speech as president of the Chartered Institute of Marketing, Billy Hastings attacked government policies which concentrated investment on industries which tended to have a shorter life cycle, rather than supporting the longer term benefits of tourism. He insisted that they concentrate their efforts on catering for tourists whom he described as being as important to Ireland as oil was to the Middle East. It was time to break down barriers and parochialism and 'think big'. The words sank home, especially as they had come from such a pillar of respected society. Civil servants and government ministers began to take notice and concentrate some of their efforts on support for the hotel industry.

A New Era

A decision was taken to close the Europa for six months to enable repairs and renovations to be carried out. There was little choice since the building had been destroyed beyond use as a hotel. To complete the repair work the hotel closed during the middle of August 1993, not to reopen until the end of January 1994. Only three staff members remained in post – Michael Williamson, to smooth out any administration matters and to complete inventories and mothball equipment; Carolyn Stalker, to look after the telephones and mail and Stephen Carson, to look after general security. The remainder of the

Belfast. He replied by saying that the closure was not bad news, but on the contrary, should be seen as the beginning of a new and exciting chapter in the hotel's history – a sentiment which was endorsed by the Hastings Group directors.

Plans were already being drawn up to completely refurbish the hotel, with Billy Hastings vowing to transform the battered exterior of the building and return the Europa to those happier days when it had boasted its own penthouse suite and a corps of chefs whose food would have satisfied the most sophisticated of palates anywhere in the world. Resident guests, many of whom were loyal customers of the Europa, were found alternative accommodation, many of whom were loyal customers of the Europa. He planned to reopen the popular 'Paradise Lost' nightclub within six weeks and hoped that, by 1 February 1994, the new dining and banqueting areas and the bedrooms would be ready for occupation once more. The cost of the lavish upgrading was budgeted to be in the region of £4 million.

Billy Hastings was now in his element. He had in his ownership the one hotel he had always coveted. He was determined to make the best use of this wonderful hotel and was enthusiastic about its infinite possibilities. As a leading Irish hotelier at the time, Billy was in an excellent position to promote his Belfast city centre jewel and thus become the number one hotelier in Northern Ireland. He would turn the Europa into one of the finest hotels in Ireland having, first of all, brushed aside the pessimistic remarks made by local journalists who interviewed him in the early days after his purchase of the Europa. They had asked him why he wanted to own 'the most bombed hotel' in town, to which he responded that many of the stories about the Europa's problems were inconsequential and often downright wrong. The hotel was central in Belfast and was in the best situation anywhere in Northern Ireland. He would turn it into the flagship hotel of the

American tourist, Teresa Bahoc, leaving the hotel prior to its closure for refurbishment

employees were either relocated to other hotels within the Group or were reluctantly made redundant. Many were then contacted to restart the following January although a number had found other jobs in the interim.

Michael Williamson was interviewed by the press and asked if the closure of the Europa was bad news for

Province. When he had committed the funds to revitalise the Europa he had already invested over £30 million in the hotel industry in Northern Ireland since 1972. When asked what help the government had given him for improving facilities for the hotel trade, he said that he had received about £100,000 – an amount which seemed quite derisory in the circumstances.

A Stunning New Design

The chief objective of the architects, Robinson Patterson Partnership, was to radically change the 1970s image of the Europa into something akin to the style of one of the grand Parisian hotels of the early years of the 20th century. It was a stunning design made to last.

In their presentation to the Hastings board, the architects outlined four options for the refurbishment of the hotel. The Europa could be turned into offices after a straightforward repair. It could be turned into a 3 star hotel which had the advantage of a speedy resolution although it would be impossible to solve the hotel's image problem. The third option was to turn it into a 4 star hotel which the architects and Billy favoured most of all. The final option was for it to become a 5 star establishment. This would have been too expensive even allowing for very much improved facilities. There were, in their professional estimation, many advantages in choosing the four star plan. Generally the hotel, with its timeless classical design, would be depicted as classy, clubby and with a 'here to stay' image. The improvements

Architect's drawing of the new Europa exterior

83

were stunning and imaginative – Billy Hastings and his fellow directors fully endorsed the recommendations.

With the exterior of the building clad in a granite-based stone, and the interior resplendent in marble and the finest quality timber, the principal architect, George Robinson, assisted by the builders, Grahams of Dromore, promised a building which would be timeless and elegant when completed – a promise which they clearly delivered. It was agreed that the new entrance was its most elegant feature. Grand hotels needed grand entrances.

An arcade of ten metre high columns was erected leading into a central rotunda which formed a large circular space rising from the reception area up to the first floor level. The doors and desks were made of stained cherry wood and the rich red colour gave warmth to the interior. Another innovation incorporated into the design was the Opera Room, a private dining facility for up to eight people within the Gallery restaurant. Its intimacy and original artworks by local artist, Robert Bottom, offered the opportunity for dinner party style dining within a contemporary restaurant setting.

The new exterior under construction

The entire second floor of bedrooms was decommissioned to make way for the impressive new Eurobusiness Centre which

was able to accommodate up to 200 delegates in superbly appointed, state-of-the-art meeting rooms in the most luxurious surroundings. The excellent facilities were similar to those which had recently been opened at the Confex Centre in the Stormont Hotel. Not only were the suites suitable for seminars and conferences, but they could also host lunch and dinner parties, or provide corporate hospitality for those attending performances in the Grand Opera House next door.

The most striking room in the new centre was, however, the perfectly circular room directly above the entrance foyer, known as the Rotunda. In this elegant and unusual room, up to thirty people could dine around a circular table where egalitarian seating plans were considered important. The publicity material provided at the time of the opening of these facilities aptly summed up the excellence on offer – 'Quality exudes from every detail whether it be the smart reception, stylish rooms or the stunning atrium with views over Great Victoria Street'.

The first phase of refurbishment was finished by February 1994 when the 184 bedrooms were reopened complete with double glazed windows, king sized beds and fine new bathrooms installed with new fittings and carpet. Five luxury suites were also constructed out of ten existing bedrooms. The magnificent new Grand Ballroom, built in Emerald days, was the *piece de resistance*. It was capable of holding up to 1,000 people in theatre style conferences or it could be adapted into five large syndicate rooms. Reputed to be the largest function room anywhere in Northern Ireland, the area could also be turned into a banqueting hall for 700 guests.

The original budget of around £4 million was exceeded and the final bill for refurbishment was almost £6 million. By having the foresight to undertake these creative renovations, the Hastings Group had demonstrated its

The luxurious new Europa exterior prior to reopening

belief in the future –not just restoring the hotel as it had been but raising it to a very fine four star hotel. The directors had given Belfast the top class hotel it deserved.

Work proceeded apace and it was not long before the ground floor extension was completed with its high ceiling and its lobby bar, reception area and shop. The staff were particularly pleased and proud when the new 20 hour Brasserie opened, to serve the public from 6 a.m. through to 2 a.m. It provided excellent food, cooked by the finest chefs available. Customers were attended by waiters who now had sophisticated electronic equipment available to relay their orders instantaneously to the kitchens.

Prospects of Peace

Billy Hastings' faith in buying the Europa in a dilapidated state when life in Northern Ireland was still greatly troubled was richly rewarded when the ceasefires called by

The Eurobusiness Centre, the Grand Ballroom and the Gallery Lounge

the IRA at the end of August 1994, followed in October by Loyalist paramilitaries, came into operation. After over twenty five years of senseless violence, the people of the Province could breathe a sigh of relief. Many of the younger citizens had not, of course, known anything other than violence throughout their lives. There was no city centre night life, little entertainment and very few nightclubs and restaurants. Any cinemas which existed were far away in the suburbs. The time had come for everyone to throw off the shackles of doom and despair and live again.

With the wonderfully refurbished Europa Hotel in the midst of this rejoicing it showed the public that the optimistic approach to restoring such a city centre icon had paid off handsomely. Before long the scaffolding was removed revealing the stunning new Grecian columns and, at night, the hotel's central spine was lit up in green with the name 'Europa' etched out in 30 foot letters in an unusual shade of deep red. The hotel's neon sign on the roof could now be seen from all parts of the city, north, east, south and west. For the first time, guests could enter the hotel without having to pass through the unsightly security hut, a feature that the new Europa was happy to dispense with.

The new general manager, John Toner, with Michael Williamson now as assistant general manager, had over 90 fulltime staff back on duty and he confidently predicted that there would be 160 employees by the time the hotel became fully functional in November. The Europa was back in business; Belfast was back in business and Northern Ireland could look forward to peace and prosperity – at long last. Importantly, too, the Europa had long since ceased to hold the 'most bombed hotel in Europe' tag. The Holiday Inn in Sarajevo now held that dubious accolade. The symbolism of the Europa's spectacular revival was central to the spirit of confidence that everywhere abounded.

Penny Thornberry, then the Europa's sales manager, recalled that there were, at that time, no other city centre hotels in Belfast. Yet the Europa could command top rates for customers although they had to enter through a side door owing to the on-going building work. There were not even any carpets on the floors for a time and breakfast had to be served on the top floor. The customers were, however, still happy to be there paying 1994 prices, higher than can be achieved today because of increased competition in the city.

A Grand Reopening or Two

The new style Europa had not one, but two reopenings. The first took place on 4 February 1994, barely nine months after the bomb blast the previous May. As the workmen were leaving the hotel premises that evening, the first guests for the grand charity ball for the Flax Trust, a north Belfast enterprise agency, were eagerly streaming in to enjoy a feast of food and entertainment. Five hundred diners sat down to an excellent meal. Sixteen chefs were on duty preparing 300 lbs of prime sirloin steak, 600 lbs of potatoes, 140 lbs of broccoli and more than 2,000 profiteroles for that first banquet of the Europa's new era. The evening was an outstanding success and the hotel had been well and truly relaunched.

Although the hotel had been taking guests over the late summer months, the Europa was not officially and finally reopened until 18 October 1994. John Toner told the waiting journalists that the Europa was 'back from the blast and making its 22nd comeback'.

In December 1994 the Industrial Development Board held an Investors' Forum based at the Europa. The conference and banquet were attended by many United States and British business leaders, hosted by the then Prime Minister, John Major. This was an important endorsement for Belfast and an auspicious start for the Europa. It was a mark of returning normality that the Prime Minister felt confident enough in the security situation to back such an event. The United States Secretary for Commerce, Ron Brown, lent his considerable political weight to the proceedings and the EU Commissioner, Carlos Troijan, used the occasion to launch a £50 million EU Peace and Reconciliation funding package for Northern Ireland. All in all it proved to be a glittering event and proof positive of the government's determination to use the signs of normality, as evidenced by the Europa's return to operation, to try and ensure the development of what became known as the 'peace process'.

Bookings for the coming Christmas season were flooding in and, best of all news, a significant number of enquiries from Republic of Ireland tour bus operators were being made to include Northern Ireland on their tour itineraries once again. Howard Hastings, then operations director, said how important this breakthrough would be when many local hotels and tourist outlets had almost forgotten what a tour bus looked like. The Europa would now benefit from the long awaited tourist boom by offering bed and breakfast in a single room during the week for £89 and at the weekends for as low as £44, with a double room costing £120 and £60 respectively. Happier days hopefully now lay ahead, not just for the Europa, but also for the

A breathtaking view of Belfast

for up to 9%. The Republic had 80,000 people employed in the sector whilst Northern Ireland had just 9,000. The forecasts looked good with a significant additional number of people becoming engaged in the hotel and hospitality trade. Signs for an upturn in fortunes looked promising.

The Irish government stepped in to lend its support to the prospective bonanza in the north. The then Trade Minister, Enda Kenny, commissioned a report to give advice as to what additional resources were needed to assist the resurgent economies in both parts of the island. The Northern Ireland Tourist Board was convinced that tourism would virtually double in the ensuing few years and recommended more and more accommodation to cope with the upsurge. The fact, then, that Hastings Hotels were right in the middle of this healthy competition augured well for visitors to Northern Ireland.

Whilst the Europa was well placed to benefit from the boom, other influential hotel 'brand' names, as predicted, began to set up shop in the Province in direct opposition to Hastings Hotels. The arrival of the more famous names and 'brands' held no fear for the Hastings organisation. Julie Maguire, Billy's daughter and the firm's marketing

many other restaurants and shops located on Belfast's Golden Mile.

Looking Forward to a Confident Future

Whilst the Europa was being once again fully booked and its restaurants and bars filled to capacity, even more optimistic reports on trade and tourism in Northern Ireland were being published. Analysts were confidently projecting that as many as 20,000 new jobs would be created in the tourism industry in the foreseeable future to benefit from the peace dividend. Before the ceasefires only 2% of Northern Ireland's Gross National Product was associated with tourism. In the Republic it accounted director, said that the ceasefire and the new investment would benefit the whole industry. The cessation of violence after such a long and tortuous period was being likened to the fall of the Berlin wall. It was an apt comparison.

There was yet more good news for the Hastings Hotels Group. The Group revealed a dramatic jump in its annual profits. In the year 1995 they were doubled to a pre-tax figure of over £2.5 million, a rise of 167% over the profits from the previous year. The improved financial activity was due to the intense period of activity surrounding the visit of President Clinton in late 1995; nonetheless, the improved financial situation boosted the Group's confidence at a time when its balance sheet was severely stretched after the purchase and refurbishment of the Europa.

An American President comes to stay

An American President's visit represents one of the biggest coups ever achieved by any private commercial enterprise. Deciding to stay in the city's premier hotel rather than in the safety and quiet of the Governor's former official residence at Hillsborough Castle spoke volumes. Not only did the President want to live where the people lived – in the midst of their own capital city – but there was also a hotel organisation willing to accept a challenge of considerable magnitude.

The visit and stay at the Europa by President and Mrs Clinton was the ideal opportunity to prove, once and for all, that the Hastings empire could and would provide services second to none for such VIPs.

By the end of November 1995, the ceasefires had been in operation for over a year. Whilst life had very much returned to normal there were still issues which were giving the politicians, both at Westminster and locally in Northern Ireland, some cause for concern. The peace process was still decidedly shaky. When it became known that President William Jefferson Clinton had indicated his desire to come to Ireland with a view to using his good offices to copper fasten the cessation of violence, those in authority jumped at the chance to see how best he could do it.

Both the Conservative British Prime Minister, John Major, and the Irish Taoiseach, John Bruton, who had been meeting and

President Clinton's personalised photograph to Martin Mulholland, head concierge

To Martin Mulholland With Appreciation, Bill Clinton

uniquely detailed and members of his administration staff need to be in situ, as was the case for those who stayed at the Europa, for eight weeks in advance.

As part of his European tour, President Clinton was scheduled to spend time in London, Belfast and Dublin. In the first instance he arrived in London for talks with the British Prime Minister and then he delivered an address to both Houses of Parliament before taking tea with the Queen.

The Presidential Party arrives in Northern Ireland

The first ever visit by a serving American President to Northern Ireland took place on 30 November 1995. Just after nine o'clock on a grey morning, Air Force One landed at Belfast International Airport. The Presidential motorcade sped in to Belfast along the motorway which had been closed to the public for the duration. The President made whirlwind tours of west Belfast where he stopped to speak to the locals on the Shankill and Falls Roads; delivered an outstanding speech at the Mackie factory on the Springfield Road; spent time in Londonderry, supported by John Hume MEP, Phil Coulter and other prominent citizens, wooing the people of the Maiden City, before finally arriving at the Europa Hotel to make ready for the big event of the evening.

Cheering crowds greeted the Clintons at every engagement. This one day visit, a challenge for the local

Air Force One arriving at Belfast International Airport

talking about the future of Northern Ireland for some time, saw the distinct advantages of a visit by President Clinton and they were able to conclude more of their 'twin track' discussions just in advance of the visit. The scene was set. The President would be coming to help broker a watertight deal to ensure the continuance of the ceasefires. London, Belfast and Dublin started to make their preparations. And when it was decided that the Clintons (as Mrs Hillary Clinton had also agreed to join her husband) had insisted that they stay for part of their visit in Belfast, the diplomatic wheels rolled into action. Where would they stay? What people would they meet? Which parts of the Province would they visit? When an American President travels abroad, the planning process is media, gathered momentum at each Presidential stop. By early evening excitement had reached fever pitch. People were wondering where they would position themselves on a night such as this. As the honoured guests arrived at the Europa, thousands upon thousands of people were walking from all parts of the city to converge on the City Hall to witness the most powerful man in the world switch on the city's Christmas tree lights.

Arrival at the Europa

For the staff at the Europa, the wait was over. Their extensive preparations had been completed and all that was left to be done was to extend the hand of friendship to President and Mrs Clinton as they stepped over the hotel threshold that Thursday evening. For the

The President's motorcade making its way through the streets of Belfast

Allyson Hastings and Julie Maguire with President Clinton

had brought the President's own personal staff to look after him. Only six of the hotel staff, headed by John Toner, were temporarily attached to him. Three entire floors, the 9th, 10th and 11th, had been taken over by the President's entourage and the Clintons themselves were accommodated in one of the hotel's five luxury suites, number 1011, which had had bullet proof windows installed. The bedroom next door, number 1009, was required for the two secret servicemen whose duty it was to look after the twenty three suitcases of luggage which the Clintons had brought with them. They also doubled as their dressers. According to John Toner, his VIPs had been model guests and had requested nothing more remarkable than some foam pillows, a few extra towels and a big mug for the President. One of the Europa's waiters had a close encounter with one

President Clinton greets Martin Mulholland

next few hours the Belfast Europa became the White House. A switchboard, manned by United States personnel, was set up in the hotel and calls for the President of the United States were dealt with, not in Washington, D.C., but in Belfast, Northern Ireland. Telephones were answered with the words 'White House, Belfast, how may I help you?' The American secret service staff had already turned over every corner of the building. No security detail had been overlooked. They had taken over the Grand Ballroom for the use of their press corps and in this room was also housed the 'red button' which would be used in the event of a Presidential order to launch a nuclear attack.

Although the American secret service staff had expressed their satisfaction at all the proposed arrangements, they

of the American secret servicemen. As he entered the lift, he realised that the other person inside was a member of the Presidential staff. There was no mistaking the black coat and dark glasses. Although a little nervous, the waiter tried to make conversation and, remembering a line from the film 'Pulp Fiction', turned to the American and asked him if he was 'carrying the red apples'. With a movement which caught the waiter a little by surprise, the secret serviceman opened his coat just wide enough to reveal two 9mm regulation handguns. He did not know where to look and was saved by the bell when the lift opened at his floor. He practically leapt out into the hall without taking a moment to look back!

White House staff had originally asked for exclusive use of the hotel for the duration of the Clintons' stay. However there was an existing booking from one of the hotel's regular clients, Shorts (now Bombardier Aerospace), and the hotel insisted that the booking from such loyal customers should be honoured. After thorough security checks, the booking was permitted to remain.

During the day, before the Clintons' arrival at the Europa, an urgent telephone call had been made with a request to provide the President and his wife with a meal which would be eaten aboard a helicopter on their way to Londonderry. Given just twenty minutes' notice, the executive chef, Gerry Rosato, came up trumps and had the light meal, consisting of Ulster coddle broth, wild Irish salmon and Armagh apple pie, delivered to the City Airport within the specified time. The breakfast delivered to them on the Friday morning was American style – orange juice, herbal tea and bagels. The food which the Clintons ate at the hotel was, of course, carefully scrutinised by the ubiquitous secret service personnel but everything was declared to be in order – and of top quality, as befitted the top rate chefs in the Europa kitchen.

The Clintons received gifts from the hotel staff which were presented by head concierge, Martin Mulholland. A painting by a local artist of him drinking a pint of Guinness was presented to the President and both he and his wife also received personalised bathrobes. Many other gifts such as linen, knitwear, whiskey, crystal and pottery from other Belfast businesses arrived all day long for the Clintons. Twenty sacks full of fan mail were also delivered during the day. When they left the hotel the special visitors thanked the hotel staff profusely for their kind attention to every detail associated with their short visit. The President confided in them that he had been excited at the prospect of overnighting at the Europa in Belfast although his advisors had been more cautious about the idea.

He felt vindicated at his decision given the wonderful reception he had received everywhere he had visited. Their own personnel had reportedly said that this had been the President's most successful trip

David Trimble, official Ulster Unionist leader, with President Clinton at Queen's University

best advertisement for the city's new found confidence. President Clinton had sent out the strongest possible message that Northern Ireland had been completely transformed and was now the place for further investment. The visit had brought much needed prosperity to Belfast and to the entire Province.

The Main Event

Putting aside the excellent reception afforded to the Clintons at the Europa, the chief event of that Thursday evening in Belfast was the switching on of the Christmas tree lights and the speeches to be made to the assembled crowds gathered around the majestic Belfast City Hall. Estimates of the size of the crowd greatly differed. Some said 50,000 and others twice that figure. What was not in question, however, was the enthusiasm of those expectant throngs as they awaited the President's arrival on to the bullet-screen protected podium. It was a chill late November evening but this did not dampen the fervour of those assembled for they had, in the meantime, been magnificently entertained by Van Morrison and Brian Kennedy.

President Clinton addressing the crowds gathered at Belfast City Hall after switching on the city's Christmas lights

abroad. This assertion had been calculated to flatter – and it certainly did. For a United States President to have stayed in the reputed 'most bombed hotel anywhere' sent a loud and clear picture throughout the world. Belfast was a great place to stay and the Europa Hotel was the

Bill Clinton told the people of Belfast how much he had enjoyed his brief visit and how momentous it was to begin his Christmas season in Belfast. He said how much this long-awaited peace would bring change to the lives of everyone and that message hit a chord in the hearts of his entire audience. He told them that the visit to Northern Ireland was one of the most important and most thrilling he had ever undertaken. He would remember the day for as long as he lived with great gratitude.

The Legacy of the President's Visit

President Bill Clinton had left an indelible mark on the fabric of Northern Irish society following his historic, yet all too brief, stay in the Province. He had come as a peacemaker and had touched the hearts of many people on both sides of a once divided society. Even on his departure from the Europa he had ordered his car to stop to allow him to say farewell to the crowds who had gathered to bid him 'bon voyage'.

Secret service minders had been horrified at this impromptu walkabout in Glengall Street at the side door of the Europa as he pressed flesh and kissed babies.

Above all, the visit had paved the way for further investment in the Province to consolidate the peace dividend. The demons had finally been laid to rest.

The Clinton Suite

The company directors and the staff at the Europa were determined to commemorate the visit to their hotel by the United States President. Hardly had the Clintons left, therefore, than it was decided to give a new name to room 1011. The suite consisted of a bedroom with a super king sized bed, a lounge area and a bathroom complete with bath and shower. It would become styled as 'The Clinton Suite'. It became popular with visiting Americans who felt honoured to be sleeping in the bedroom once used by President and Mrs Clinton.

The official opening of 'The Clinton Suite' did not, however, take place until 1 July 1996. It was frequently asked at the time why such an American

The Clinton Suite

Billy Hastings, Doug Heady, American Consul Kathleen Stevens and John Toner at the official opening of the Clinton Suite

served with President Clinton and First Lady cocktails. The President's cocktail consisted of vodka and cranberry juice with a slice of lime. The First Lady's had the same principal ingredients but with a splash of orange juice. Following an address by the American Consul, Ms Kathleen Stephens, in which she praised the hotel staff for the high standards provided for the presidential party, and speeches from other VIPs, the invited guests were taken to the suite itself. There the Consul unveiled a plaque in the room and then the remaining guests were given a conducted tour of the suite and shown the various items of memorabilia that singled out the rooms as something forever special. There was an American flag, which had been flying at the White House during the President's visit to Northern Ireland, taking pride of place above the bed. The Arkansas State Flag from Bill Clinton's home state, where he had been Governor, also adorned the walls of the room. Other touches included a signed photograph of Bill and Hillary Clinton and a framed biography of the President. The price of the suite was £300 per night and, according to Doug Heady, the suite continues to be in constant demand and occupation.

event had not taken place on Independence Day – the 4th of July. The answer was simple enough. The American Consulate in Belfast had a number of pre-arranged parties and gatherings that day and Doug Heady, the United States-born deputy general manager of the Europa at that time, who was arranging the special day, wanted to ensure that their suite dedication would be the big event of their day – the 1st of July.

Invitations were sent out 'cordially inviting guests to the formal dedication of the President Bill Clinton Suite'. Arrangements for the day began over a month in advance and a programme for the day was drawn up. It was to be an impressive occasion. On arrival all the VIPs were

On returning downstairs, the guests and members of the press corps were treated to an all-American lunch consisting of hot dogs, pizza, baked beans, potato salad, coleslaw, tortilla chips and salsa. The theme of the meal was the representation of a typical New York street corner with people walking along and grabbing a bite to eat. Considering that this 'fast food' was not the usual Europa fare, nonetheless it went down well with the honoured guests. This themed idea turned out to be a great success and an identical menu was made available in the Brasserie and the Gallery restaurants for all other customers in the hotel that day.

In the evening the programme continued with an American Blues Night in the Lobby Bar with Ireland's leading Blues band quintet, Blues Experience. During this part of the proceedings the newly donated President's Prize was announced. Through the generosity of British Telecom, who provided the funds, the prize was to be competed for by children from both sides of the community. A winner from each tradition was then to be sent off to America to take part in a cultural exchange programme.

OFFICE OF
WILLIAM JEFFERSON CLINTON

A Special Message from the White House to the Staff at the Europa

Some years later, on 15 May 2002, a very special letter arrived for the staff at the Europa. Enclosed in a gold embossed envelope marked 'The White House', came a message from President Clinton to all the men and women on the Europa staff who, despite profound adversity, had continued to work for the success of the hotel. Reminding them that Ireland had suffered bloodshed and unending violence over the past century, he went on to say that the new century had begun with the best hope for peace in Ireland during their lifetimes. His optimism regarding the resilience, courage, vision and indomitable spirit for which the Irish had always been known was reflected in his heartfelt letter. The entire staff felt proud to have been the recipients of such a fine tribute from the President who had stayed amongst them back in 1995. The letter takes pride of place amongst mementoes sent to the hotel by visiting VIPs.

Brighter Europa Days

The Clintons' visit had fulfilled the Europa's wildest expectations. Hotel occupancy increased from the low 50% base at the time of the hotel's purchase in 1993 to an impressive 80% early in 1996. The Clinton factor was proving a great boost not only to the Europa but also to all businesses in Belfast. During 1995 as a whole, figures for holidaymakers throughout Northern Ireland had risen by 56% to almost half a million people. Hoteliers were holding their breath in the hope that the ceasefires would prevail and that the Province would return to complete normality.

General de Chastelain and Jeanne Rankin enjoy a meal at the Europa

However, by the beginning of 1996, not long after the President's visit, the white tapes were sealing off the Europa once more. The resultant disruption caused by this bomb hoax made people nervous and apprehensive. The ceasefires had, by now, broken down and the huge explosions in London at Canary

Wharf on 9 February 1996 had dampened the ardour of even the most optimistic. Yet Billy Hastings, in an interview soon after the Europa's latest threat, remained upbeat. He was extremely hopeful that, despite the breakdown of the ceasefires,

business would continue to increase in the hotel and tourist industry. Tour bookings and hotel reservations had reached an unprecedented level never before seen in Northern Ireland.

To mark the first anniversary of

the Clintons' stay at the Europa, Senator George Mitchell, who chaired the ongoing peace negotiations, was invited to the Europa on 27 November 1996 to unveil a portrait of the President. The painting by young Belfast artist, Nicola Russell, had been

specially commissioned by the Europa Hotel. As he addressed the assembled guests at the ceremony, Senator Mitchell commended the artist on her portrait, ruefully suggesting that perhaps she could paint his own portrait, if he could be shown as being as

Cooking up a Storm

and that the Province would ... late normality.

Hastings, in an interview soon after the Europa's latest threat, remained upbeat. He was

Chapter 6

Brighter Europa Days

The Clintons' visit had fulfilled the Europa's wildest expectations. Hotel occupancy increased from the low 50% base at the time of the hotel's purchase in 1993 to an impressive 80% early in 1996. The Clinton factor was proving a great boost not only to the Europa but also to all businesses in Belfast. During 1995 as a whole, figures for holidaymakers throughout Northern Ireland had risen by 56% to almost half a million people. Hoteliers were holding their breath in the hope that the ceasefires would prevail and that the Province would return to complete normality.

However, by the beginning of 1996, not long after the President's visit, the white tapes were sealing off the Europa once more. The resultant disruption caused by this bomb hoax made people nervous and apprehensive. The ceasefires had, by now, broken down and the huge explosions in London at Canary Wharf on 9 February 1996 had dampened the ardour of even the most optimistic. Yet Billy Hastings, in an interview soon after the Europa's latest threat, remained upbeat. He was extremely hopeful that, despite the breakdown of the ceasefires, business would continue to increase in the hotel and tourist industry. Tour bookings and hotel reservations had reached an unprecedented level in Northern Ireland.

To mark the first anniversary of the Clintons' stay at the Europa, Senator George Mitchell, who chaired the ongoing peace negotiations, was invited to the Europa on 27 November 1996 to unveil a portrait of the President. The painting by young Belfast artist, Nicola Russell, had been specially commissioned by the Europa Hotel. As he addressed the assembled guests at the ceremony, Senator Mitchell commended the artist on her portrait, ruefully suggesting that perhaps she could paint his own portrait, if he could be shown as being as young looking as President Clinton!

Senator Mitchell was, at that time, spending much of his life at the Europa and, in fact, described himself as a semi-permanent resident of the hotel. He usually addressed Billy Hastings as his landlord! He stayed at the hotel, on and off, for well over three years. One eleventh of July he was in the hotel and wanted to find out what went on the night before the notorious Twelfth of July. He was told about the bonfire tradition and promptly left the hotel on his own and walked over to Sandy Row – one of Belfast's most infamous hot spots, especially on the eleventh of July. The staff were naturally a little apprehensive about such an important visitor stepping out to witness the goings-on around a monster bonfire. They need not have worried for when Senator Mitchell returned, there was a smile on his face. He had

General John de Chastelain

not only enjoyed what he had seen but had even spoken to some of the locals. One wonders what sort of conversation had taken place between this progenitor of peace and those who were enjoying their traditional bonfire night!

Senator Mitchell's fellow peace negotiator, the Canadian general, John de Chastelain, was also a guest for something over four years, which included his time in charge of the arms decommissioning body. In June 2003 General de Chastelain sent this message to the staff of the Europa.

From General John de Chastelain

I first stayed at the Europa Hotel in December 1995 when the former Senator George Mitchell, the former Prime Minister Harri Holkeri and I came to Belfast as members of the International Body conducting an examination into the decommissioning of paramilitary arms. The Body had a mandate to report to the two Governments by the middle of January 1996 and our stay in Belfast was not expected to be long.

I had not been in Belfast before, and the circuitous route taken by the cars that brought us to town from the airport gave me the impression that the hotel was at the centre of the commercial core of the city. That impression was heightened by the Europa's proximity to the railway station and bus terminal, the Opera House and the Crown Pub, and by the impressive continental nature of its façade, and the busy flow of traffic up and down Great Victoria Street.

I had heard of the Europa's history during the period of the 'Troubles' and how it had continued to operate despite bombings and intimidation, and how it provided a centre where members of the media had gathered when covering the action on the streets.

The International Body publicised its report at a press conference in the Europa's upper Conference Hall in mid-January 1996 and the Body was disbanded. I had enjoyed the brief time we stayed at the hotel, but I had no reason to believe I would see it again. However, when Mitchell, Holkeri and I were invited back five months later, in June 1996, to chair certain aspects of the talks to re-establish a permanent peace in Northern Ireland, it was to the Europa that we returned. The hotel was to become our home over the next two years.

With the advent of the Belfast or Good Friday Agreement on April 10th 1998, the Office of the Independent Chairman dissolved. George Mitchell, Harri Holkeri and their staffs returned home, but I remained, having already become part of the Commission mandated to effect the decommissioning aspects of the Agreement.

Off and on, I had been at the Europa from December 1995 to February 1999, although my time there involved much coming and going. The hotel was kind enough to assign me to the same room each time I stayed, and in many ways it became a second home. I took most of my meals in the Brasserie and I got to know many of the staff there and at the front desk. In time, I got to know well the proprietor of the Hastings chain of hotels, Dr. Billy Hastings, as I did the Manager, John Toner, and the Front Desk Manager, Carolyn Stalker.

Since I have been involved in Northern Ireland – and at the time of writing I am still involved there – I have been much impressed by the warmth and hospitality of the people and the welcome they give to strangers like me. This was nowhere more true than of my stay at the Europa and my relationship with the members of its staff. It is indeed a great hotel, and long may it prosper.

Teachers, Actors and Showbiz Entertainers

Another of the Europa's notable coups was in attracting the Irish National Teachers Organisation (INTO) to use the hotel for its annual conference in November 1996. INTO had not crossed the border since 1955 and when they realised what the Europa could offer they booked in and were delighted with the result. Eight hundred delegates were able to sample the facilities provided by the Europa. They were pleased, for example, that the hotel staff could serve lunch to everyone in less than an hour which meant more time in conference. The decision by management to designate hotel staff to be in constant attendance on the delegates, proved to be a particular success. If a problem arose with the overhead projectors, for instance, then the staff member was on hand to rectify the problem immediately. The fact that the entire 800 delegates sat down to dinner in the evening highlighted their confidence in the Europa's attention to every detail and, for those who had come up from the south, it added to the novelty value to be able to return to their homes to say that they had eaten a superb meal in the Belfast Europa.

The Europa Hotel became the venue for one very popular event during the 1997 Belfast Festival at Queen's. In the hotel's penthouse theatre, the well known Roma Tomelty put on a most successful production of Neil Simon's hilarious comedy, 'Last of the Red Hot Lovers'. It

Howard Hastings (second left) with performers from the Hastings Ulster Cabaret at the Europa, 1996

A view of the Europa along Franklin Street

proved so popular that extra performances had to be slotted in on Sunday afternoons. Discerning patrons had found a new venue and they had enjoyed it. Reviews of the show were outstanding and the fact that the Europa had been used for this type of entertainment meant that the hotel was able to attract customers who otherwise might not have considered it as a potential location for a meal.

On 9 December the *Belfast Telegraph* staged the annual Sports Star of the Year awards at the Europa. Again it proved a wise choice of venue. The staff, under John Toner, excelled in not only preparing the banqueting hall for the ceremony but also in providing a waiter service second to none. That year the winner of the coveted prize was the jockey, Tony McCoy, although many other local stars from every sport from hockey to rugby football were also presented with their own awards.

Martin Mulholland, head concierge

Ireland's popular boy band, Boyzone, spent time at the Europa after delighting their fans with their slick dance routines and number one hit songs in Belfast's Waterfront Hall. The hotel staff, although well used to looking after celebrity guests, found some difficulty in keeping the band's excited fans away from the front doors of the

Paddy McAnerney, head barman

Europa. They were eventually able to bundle the pop stars out of a side exit into their waiting limousine.

During the mid 1990s, the actress, Julia Roberts had a much publicised affair with the actor, Jason Patric, whilst at the same time dating Kiefer Sutherland. So they decided to run away to Ireland to avoid the media frenzy. At the Europa, Martin Mulholland, the head concierge, received an urgent phone call asking him to go to the back door of the hotel as there were VIPs who needed to be checked in very privately. He was surprised, to say the least, to find Julia and Jason there and hurriedly brought them inside. After settling in, they went off to Paul Rankin's restaurant, Roscoff, for a quiet meal. However they were spotted there and it was not long before the press arrived. Another frantic call was made to Martin at the Europa who was on hand to organise a taxi driver - known both to Martin and the actors - to whisk them off to Dublin. Unfortunately they were not able to overnight at the Europa but they later made contact with the hotel to thank Martin for his help and presence of mind.

Although the Europa is 180 feet high, it was commonplace, especially during the late 1990s, to see many intrepid men and women abseiling from the roof down into Great Victoria Street below to raise money for various worthy charities. For many of the participants, it was their first attempt at this very scary activity. Included in those who dared – and succeeded – in reaching the ground safely were David Taylor, the financial controller of Nambarrie Tea and Allyson Hastings, the director of events for the Hastings Group. They were heard to say on completing their jump 'The hard bit is getting over the edge, the rest is just plain abseiling!'

Recognition for Europa Staff

Whilst the Europa staff went about their business of making their guests feel relaxed and comfortable inside the hotel, many of them were achieving success for their contributions outside in the wider world of catering and tourism.

In March 1995, Martin Mulholland, the head concierge, received his 'golden keys', the badge of membership of the exclusive 'Les Clefs d'Or'. He had gained entry to this prestigious international association of hall porters by being nominated by existing members. He became the first recipient in Northern Ireland since Jimmy Connor some years previously. In late 1996, the head barman at the Europa, Paddy McAnerney, beat off intense competition to become Bartender of the Year. At the same event, John Toner was selected as Northern Ireland's Professional Manager of the Year, and Heather McCrory won the Receptionist of the Year award.

At a reception in Hillsborough Castle in October 1996, the economy minister, Baroness Denton, presented the annual Welcome Hosts awards for achieving success in developing tourism in face of tough opposition and in a difficult economic situation. Amongst the winners was the Europa Hotel, which reached the Gold Standard level.

Senator George Mitchell with John Toner

general manager in September 2003. An already heady evening was capped for the Europa when John Toner was called upon to collect the award made to the Europa Hotel team for their high quality of staff and customer care.

John Toner, the Europa Hotel's Award Winning General Manager

John Toner, the general manager until September 2003, has been a regular recipient of top notch awards. Throughout his long years in the hotel business, John has won hospitality awards and Hotel Manager of the Year awards. As the son of a Dublin bank manager, John spent his childhood years in various homes in Newry, Warrenpoint and Downpatrick. On leaving secondary school, he successfully completed a two year catering course at Rockwell College in County Tipperary, before going to London as a trainee manager in Simpson's Hotel in the Strand. Being naturally ambitious he quickly returned to Belfast to work in the then thriving Grand Central Hotel in Royal Avenue and became senior assistant manager there.

Some time before the Grand Central closed late in 1971, John saw an advertisement in the Belfast papers seeking staff for the new Europa Hotel which was due to open in July. He was interviewed by the redoubtable Harper Brown but, although he was told he had performed well, John did not get the job. His fortunes quickly changed, however, when he was appointed general manager of the Ballyedmond Castle Hotel in Rostrevor in County Down at the age of just 22. A year later he moved to work for Hastings Hotels as general manager at the Ballygally Castle Hotel, before transferring on promotion to the Slieve Donard Hotel in Newcastle in County Down. He subsequently managed the Fir Trees Hotel in Strabane, County Tyrone, on its acquisition by the Hastings Group.

As the years rolled by more and more awards were coming the way of many of the Europa staff. In April 1998, a particularly pleasing award was presented to the chairman. Billy Hastings received the prestigious 'Lifetime Achievement Award' from the Hotel and Catering International Management Association at their Hospitality Oscars ceremony at the Europa for his valuable contribution to the hotel industry over forty years. A standing ovation from the 400 strong audience greeted the announcement, showing Billy's immense popularity amongst those who lived and worked in the trade.

At the same occasion, the Middle Manager of the Year award was made to James McGinn, who was on the Europa staff at that time and who was appointed its

Jean Francois Jamet, managing director of Guinness Ireland, presenting a print of President Clinton to John Toner which now hangs in the Lobby bar

his motto showed his commitment to treating everyone with mutual respect. 'We are ladies and gentlemen serving ladies and gentlemen' although he appreciated that it is the customers who pay the staff wages!

Being a Fellow of the Hotel and Catering International Management Association, John makes regular visits abroad to learn from hoteliers there and also, most importantly, to teach them what he knows of the hotel trade. Lessons from a manager of the Europa Hotel in Belfast are always well worth learning!

Being awarded the Hotel and Catering International Management Association's (Catey) 'Professional of the Year' award in 1988 has been his

General John de Chastelain (left) with Jeanne Rankin (right) at the launch of the Gallery Restaurant's Canadian celebration week in May 1998 with Sharon Magowan and Howard Hastings

Life as a hotel manager meant change upon change and, in 1986, after just two years in the west of the Province, he moved to Belfast to manage the Stormont Hotel near Parliament Buildings in the east of the city. Then, in 1993 when Billy Hastings had purchased the damaged Europa Hotel, he was offered the post of general manager and a directorship in recognition of his distinguished service to the Group.

John did much more than simply associate himself with the running of the Europa. He carried out his task in a skilled and consummate way and prided himself in always putting the customer first, and getting to know as many of them as he could. As happy talking to President Clinton as to any other individual visitor to the hotel,

highest accolade. This prestigious award, presented at the Grosvenor House Hotel in London, was especially significant because he was chosen by people who worked in his own field and who had appreciated his commitment. From 1999 until 2001, John was President of the Irish Hotel and Catering Institute.

John Toner's enthusiasm for the high standards which he set for the Europa and the empowering effect on his staff to think and act independently continued to benefit the hotel's customers. Six values epitomise the aims of management and staff members alike – 'we put our customers first'; 'we are professional'; 'we respect each other'; 'we work as one team'; 'we are committed to continuous improvement' and 'we achieve profit through service'.

Staff at work in the kitchen at the Europa

Food at the Europa

In such a splendid hotel as the Europa, the quality of food and the expertise of the catering staff could almost be taken for granted. Nonetheless the hotel's excellent restaurants were often visited by the world's greatest and best known connoisseurs.

The food at the hotel in the 1980s and early 1990s was excellent. In 1991, their Restaurant le 1991 was providing a pleasing dining experience and was even offering a fairly inexpensive set menu for those whose budgets might not usually have stretched to dining there.

On 12 September 1996, the Radio Ulster personalities John Bennett and Rose Neill introduced their 'Big Breakfast Show' from the Brasserie where the unsuspecting guests were asked for their candid views on the standard of cooking and service. The hotel staff were, naturally enough, somewhat nervous but their fears were soon allayed when Rose, acting as adjudicator, emerged from the restaurant with a satisfied grin on her face.

An attention-grabbing Halloween extravaganza in the hotel's Brasserie in 1997 hit the newspaper headlines. In the suitably renamed for the occasion Restaurant at the End of the Universe, the menu consisted of Arcturian pea soup and Warp Wonders followed by Cardassian trifle washed down with a Pan Galactic Gargle Blaster. The science fiction theme continued with the waiting staff dressed in their Star Trek uniforms having been beamed down to the Belfast Europa Hotel from the USS Enterprise.

The Power of Advertising

It goes without saying that for any business to succeed the advertising policy has to be of the highest quality. From

The Europa encourages Belfast to say Yes to the referendum following the Good Friday Agreement in 1998

the start the Hastings Group, under its marketing director, Julie Maguire, has been aware of the absolute necessity to produce literature which will attract customers. In this endeavour they have always achieved the best possible results. Advertising brochures are well prepared, beautifully presented and available at every tourist outlet.

Attention is paid to every detail. In many advertising publications information is translated into various languages. Useful maps of Northern Ireland, or of Belfast city centre, are included and telephone numbers and fax and email information are clearly displayed. The Europa's advertising material is kept up to date, both on the internet and as published brochures, and colourful flyers about up-and-coming one-off events are a feature of their policy.

In advertising the 'Ulster Cabaret' during the summer months of 1998, the Europa staff invited their guests 'to experience the essence of Ulster this summer at an evening dedicated to music and laughter from a host of Ulster artists, each with their own special brand of Ulster song, dance and humour, "from the land of the harp and the fiddle, the fife and the Lambeg drum".' (These words had been taken from the speech which President Clinton had made at the Mackie complex on 30 November 1995). On the reverse of the flyer, there appeared the splendid menu which included roast sirloin of Ulster beef and deep-dish Armagh apple and sultana pie.

Another popular choice for guests to the Europa was the 'evening of theatre and fine dining with the Grand Opera House and the Europa Hotel' whereby these two premier Belfast establishments came together to ensure that patrons had an unforgettable night out with their families and friends.

Nowadays each of the company's brochures is available on the Hastings Hotels website, www.hastingshotels.com, together with a wealth of additional information and services. The company has embraced modern technology by using the internet to its fullest extent in the promotion and marketing of each and every Hastings Group enterprise.

1998 – a Year of Hope and Despair

The season of Easter is a time of hope. For the entire population of Northern Ireland and the Republic and Great Britain too, Easter 1998 was a particularly auspicious occasion. The politicians were locked within the confines of Parliament Buildings at Stormont as a solution to the decades-old conflict seemed, at last, to be within their grasp. Agreement was finally hammered out in the early hours of Easter Saturday. The Belfast Agreement, more popularly named the Good Friday Agreement, had been signed by politicians of all traditions coming together to handle the affairs of Northern Ireland from Stormont once more.

Hillary Clinton arriving at the Europa for the second time

A referendum was held at the end of May, within both jurisdictions in Ireland, to give the citizens a chance to vote on the Agreement. To show the Hastings Group's unequivocal support, a 75 foot banner was lowered from the roof of the Europa with just one word inscribed thereon – 'Yes'. Howard Hastings had no qualms about displaying so prominently their advice to the public. 'The Agreement offers our best hope for economic regeneration and investment', he said, 'I hope this will be the end of visitors being afraid to come to Northern Ireland'. The referendum concluded with a large vote on both sides of the border in favour of the Agreement.

However, the Province's population was shattered to hear that a terrorist bomb had ripped through the centre of the County Tyrone town of Omagh on Saturday afternoon, 15 August 1998. Twenty nine innocent people had been killed and many more terribly injured and disfigured. Everyone came forward to help where they could. For its part, the Europa Hotel and its staff did something very practical. They offered bed and breakfast, free of charge, to any relative of those injured in the bombing who was in Belfast to visit their loved ones being treated in the city's major hospitals. To offer accommodation was a tangible way of helping in a time of need and sorrow. The hotel bedrooms were used for some considerable period by grateful relatives.

On the Eve of the Millennium

1999 was a busy and interesting year for the Europa. The previous autumn, in September 1998, Mrs Hillary Clinton had made a second visit to Belfast where she was a guest of honour at a women's conference entitled 'Vital Voices' in the Grand Opera House. During the day she used the Europa as her base and renewed her acquaintance with John Toner and his staff. On her departure Mrs Clinton was presented with an engraved crystal bowl as a reminder of this follow-up visit to Belfast. A few days later, a letter arrived for John Toner from the White House expressing Mrs. Clinton's thanks to the Europa staff for their wonderful gift and their thoughtfulness and hospitality.

The Hastings Group also decided to invest £6 million in extending the Europa by constructing a new accommodation block which would contain 56 new air-conditioned executive bedrooms. At the same time additional expenditure on both the Culloden and Stormont Hotels was announced. A total of £12 million was to be spent on the three projects. Adding these rooms at the Europa made it the largest hotel in Northern Ireland and the third biggest in Ireland. There would now be 240 rooms, further increasing the hotel's prestige and standing. Construction commenced in September 1999 and was completed before the end of the year 2000.

Staff Training

The Europa's commitment to staff training was recognised by the presentation of a new national standard award from Investors in People. By investing 5% of their staff salaries budget in training, Hastings Hotels maintained its market share in the face of growing opposition from the 'brand' hotels. At the same time the Europa attained the Republic's equivalent award – Excellence through People. It was the first Northern Ireland company to be presented with this award and only one of a small number of hotels on the island to be so awarded.

Throughout the years, too, the Europa had encouraged schools to send pupils for work experience to the Europa. In due course, the hotel reaped the benefits by being in a position to appoint many of these young people to the staff. In recent times, an important new training course has been introduced for all staff in the Hastings Group.

An outside trainer has been brought in to deliver the winning Lifetime Customers Programme utilising the Neuro Linguistic technique which helps staff to turn criticism to positive advantage. They learn to listen carefully to their patrons and to understand the different types of body language.

The Europa and the Arts

The Europa has always been a place for holding exhibitions and, of course, many ceremonies. There continue to be various wedding fairs and every kind of business exhibition. Many artists have 'got their break' at the Europa. The metal sculptor Farhad Nargol O'Neill, for example, got his first break when

Carolyn Stalker renews her acquaintance with Mrs Clinton

General de Chastelain presents John Toner and Howard Hastings with their Investor in People award

the plush reception area of the hotel and is now prominently displayed on the 12th floor of the hotel. The firm was so impressed that they produced three more of these carpets, one for each of their international showrooms to demonstrate the workmanship for which their company is renowned.

On a lighter note, the well-known game of Monopoly introduced a Northern Ireland version with the Europa featuring as a prestigious £300 property sitting alongside the Waterfront Hall and close to the Giant's Causeway.

Figures for 1999 showed a dramatic increase in the numbers of visitors to Northern Ireland to 1.6 million. The amount of money spent was £265 million and the numbers employed in the tourist industry had topped 15,000. At the Europa, as well as in the other hotels in the Group, visitor numbers had increased by 40% in four years.

he received a commission to make a metal screen for the Europa's Gallery Bar. Since that date he has fulfilled many more commissions for the Hastings Group and for other companies around the world.

Another innovation at the hotel was the commissioning of a design inspired by 17 year old student, Robyn Carson, daughter of vice chairman, Edward Carson, for a carpet depicting a map of the city of Belfast. The challenge to make the carpet was undertaken by Ulster Carpet Mills of Portadown whose workers spent three months completing the most complex and intricate carpets they had ever woven. This masterpiece until recently adorned the wall in

Staff numbers at the hotel had now risen to 155 fulltime and 145 part-time staff. This improvement in fortunes augured well for the dawn of the 21st century. A glittering New Year's Eve party to bring in the new millennium was held at the Europa. The tickets cost £199 and guests were treated to a pre-dinner sparkling wine reception; a five-course platinum service gourmet dinner prepared by the Europa's top chefs and entertainment from Peter Corry, a local star who had made his name performing in *Les Miserables* in London's West End. There was no shortage of applicants for the tickets and the year 2000 was rung in

Bill Hastings with Robyn Carson, the A level student who designed the carpet depicting a map of Belfast city centre

with much revelry at the Europa.

The stage was set for bigger and greater things for Northern Ireland's foremost hotel. Billy Hastings celebrated forty years in the catering and hotel businesses at the turn of the millennium but, rather than resting on his laurels, he is determined to work even harder, along with his fellow directors, to ensure the premier position of the Europa and the other hotels in the Group.

The Hastings Story

The grand entrance to the Slieve Donard

Billy Hastings was born in Belfast and educated at the Royal Belfast Academical Institution. His father died when he was only twelve years old and his older brother, Roy, then just seventeen, assumed total responsibility for the family's public house business in east and south Belfast.

Billy himself started his own working career with the timber firm of William Davidson and did well in the two years he worked for them. But Roy had other ideas for his able younger brother. Just after Billy's 18th birthday, Roy invited him into his office and informed him that he intended to divide the business and give him two of the public houses. His first responsibilities, therefore, were to be the Primrose Bar on the Albertbridge Road and the Deramore Arms on the Ormeau Road. But before he could settle down into his newly acquired pub empire, Billy had to learn the ropes of what was a very pressurised business. This he did in a very practical manner, working behind the bars and becoming a proficient licensee.

Although he had not exactly been born with a silver spoon in his mouth, nonetheless he did not have to seek his own way in the business world with just half a crown in his pocket. He was a second-generation businessman with his own pubs and his own responsibilities. Before long Roy and Billy had expanded their business to include three additional outlets managed on behalf of Wilson Boyd, eldest son of Samuel, who, at that time, had succeeded his father and now owned the Old Bushmills Distillery.

The young Hastings brothers' partnership flourished and, by 1953, they owned nine bars. Then tragedy struck when Roy was diagnosed with kidney disease and died at the early age of 30. Aged just 25, Billy was catapulted into the unyielding and troublesome bar trade on his own. He continued to live at home on the Upper Malone Road with his widowed mother whilst, at the same time, knowing that he could rely upon an excellent group of long established employees to keep the business afloat. But a holding operation was not part of his business ethos. His father had taught him all the essential disciplines of business and so he was determined to expand and, above all, to change the face of the trade in Belfast.

Working class bars were uninviting to many ladies and businessmen and a programme of lounge bar developments was seen as a progressive step forward at that time.

Further Expansion

Shortly after Roy's death, Billy bought The First and Last public house on the Newtownards Road from Senator Wilson Boyd. Soon afterwards he purchased the other three pubs which he had previously been managing for Senator Boyd. For these he paid £100,000, a very considerable outgoing and expense in the late 1950s. In fact Billy was shocked that Wilson Boyd had asked for such a large amount for the pubs but, in the end, Billy paid the price because he wanted to work for himself and not for someone else. He now owned thirteen public houses in working class Belfast, in the east, the south and the west of the city. At the same time he also acquired, through his latest deal with Boyd, Dundela Football ground (affectionately known as 'the Hen

The Everglades

Billy Hastings was born in Belfast and educated at the Royal Belfast Academical

Belfast.

Billy himself started his own working career with the timber firm of William Davidson and did

him that he intended to divide the business and give him two of the public houses. His first responsibilities, therefore, were to be the Primrose Bar on

Chapter 7

The Hastings Story

Billy Hastings was born in Belfast and educated at the Royal Belfast Academical Institution. His father died when he was only twelve years old and his older brother, Roy, then just seventeen, assumed total responsibility for the family's public house business in east and south Belfast.

Billy himself started his own working life with the timber firm of William Davidson and did well in the two years he worked for them. But Roy had other ideas for his able younger brother. Just after Billy's 18th birthday, Roy invited him into his office and informed him that he intended to divide the business and give him two of the public houses. His first responsibilities, therefore, were to be the Primrose Bar on the Albertbridge Road and the Deramore Arms on the Ormeau Road. But before he could settle down into his newly acquired pub empire, Billy had to learn the ropes of what was a very pressurised business. This he did in a very practical manner, working behind the bars and becoming a proficient licensee.

Although he had not exactly been born with a silver spoon in his mouth, nonetheless he did not have to seek his own way in the business world with just half a crown in his pocket. He was a second-generation businessman with his own pubs and his own responsibilities. Before long Roy and Billy had expanded their business to include three additional outlets managed on behalf of Wilson Boyd, who had succeeded his father Samuel as owner of the Old Bushmills Distillery.

The young Hastings brothers' partnership flourished and, by 1953, they owned nine bars. Then tragedy struck when Roy was diagnosed with kidney disease and died at the early age of 30. Aged just 25, Billy was catapulted into the unyielding and troublesome bar trade on his own. He continued to live at home on the Upper Malone Road with his widowed mother whilst, at the same time, knowing that he could rely upon an excellent group of long established employees to keep the business afloat. But a holding operation was not part of his business ethos. His father and brother had taught him all the essential disciplines of business and so he was determined to expand and, above all, to change the face of the trade in Belfast.

Working class bars were uninviting to many ladies and businessmen and a programme of lounge bar developments was seen as a progressive step forward at that time.

Further Expansion

Shortly after Roy's death, Billy bought The First and Last public house on the Newtownards Road from Senator Wilson Boyd. Soon afterwards he purchased the other three pubs which he had previously been managing for

Senator Boyd. For these he paid £100,000, a very considerable outgoing and expense in the late 1950s. Billy was shocked that Wilson Boyd had asked for such a large amount for the pubs, but he paid the price because he wanted to work for himself and not for someone else. He now owned thirteen public houses in working class Belfast, in the east, the south and the west of the city. At the same time he also acquired, through his latest deal with Boyd, Dundela Football ground (affectionately known as 'the Hen Run' to the locals), two houses beside the Stormont Inn and £9,000 worth of Irish whiskey under bond. Billy quickly sold the football ground to the club for £2,000 – the price he had paid for it - and they celebrated their new found independence by making him their President.

With his thirteen establishments – although some were admittedly small – he was by now one of the two largest licence holders in Northern Ireland, along with Messrs Braithwaite and McCann. On the slightly more exclusive side of the business, Lyle and Kinahan and Morton and Company were the two biggest and most established wholesalers and bottlers. In due course Lyle and Kinahan was bought by Bass Ireland; Morton and Company by the English Brewers, Thwaites; and Braithwaite and McCann was sold to individual purchasers.

The Bottling Stores and the Wholesale Business

The next – and inevitable – expansion for the Hastings enterprise was into the bottling business. It was the custom for each individual outlet to undertake its own bottling. With such an expanding business, it seemed wise to try to do the bottling in a centralised location. A store was purchased in Lord Street in east Belfast for £5,000 and the Sandown Bottling Company came into operation, giving much needed employment in the area. The intention was, of course, to supply their own outlets, with the hope and expectation that others would make use of the facility.

The premises at Lord Street were soon too small and had reached the limit of their usefulness. Subsequently an opportunity arose when the Irish Whiskey Company's Bridge End Bottling Company had also outgrown their premises. The two companies amalgamated and built a fine new property on the Ravenhill Road which they called The Ravenhill Bottling Company. Billy's partner in this exciting venture was Bill O'Hara, managing director of the Irish Whiskey Company and owner of the Royal Hotel in Bangor, County Down, and the Brown Trout Inn at Aghadowey in County Londonderry. In this new company both O'Hara and Billy Hastings owned 50% each. For some time, too, Billy was chairman of the Licensed Vintners Association and joined the Board of the Ulster Brewery Company, in which he purchased shares. This was subsequently purchased by English brewers who were eventually themselves amalgamated with Bass UK.

In order to ensure the complete success of this new bottling operation, a second-hand bottling line was purchased from a brewery in England and second-hand glass-lined cooling tanks were acquired locally from William Youngers' in Belfast. The two men then had a great slice of good fortune as they were preparing to put their new plant into operation. Carlsberg Breweries appointed the Ravenhill Bottlers as their Northern Ireland agents to import in large bulk tanks. This was an undoubted coup for Billy and his partner as it was the first time that Carlsberg had ever agreed to have their brew bottled outside Copenhagen.

This success quickly opened more doors for the company and they were soon agents for other world renowned firms like Teacher's Scotch Whisky, Gold Label Barley

Wine and many others. By 1970, they had had eight successful and profitable years in the bottling business, which had required a great deal of capital to expand. The two men had outgrown their limited financial resources and wisely decided, in the face of stiff opposition from bigger firms like Guinness and Bass Ireland, to sell out to Bass. The amount paid for the Ravenhill Bottling Company was a massive £220,000 of which Billy Hastings received £110,000. He was able, in those difficult days in Northern Ireland, to use the funds for his future businesses and the expansion of his hotels. He was appointed a director of Bass Ireland, a directorship which he held for a further 25 years.

Billy weds

In the late 1950s, Billy Hastings met Joy Hamilton. Joy had been educated at Victoria College, one of Belfast's foremost girls' schools. She rose to be Head Girl at a school she greatly loved. She passed her Senior Certificate and gained entrance to Queen's University where she successfully completed a BA degree in Modern Languages. Soon she found a job at Lisnasharragh High School in Belfast and, within her first years, was appointed head of Department. Whilst teaching there, she had as one of her French students, George Best, destined to become a Northern Ireland international football player and one of the world's finest footballers and international celebrities.

Then in 1960, aged 28, she married Billy Hastings at Drumbeg Parish church on the southern outskirts of Belfast. The couple's first home was at Harberton Park in south Belfast and there they raised their four children, Julie, Howard, Allyson and Aileen. Billy freely admits that marrying Joy was one of the smartest things he ever did in his life. Joy was more organised than he was, compared with what he has described as his own, more relaxed,

outlook to life. He worked the hardest in his life between the ages of 30 and 50, although he always has allowed himself time for home life at the weekends, a game of golf on Saturdays and church on Sunday mornings.

Moving in Different Directions

In the mid 1960s another opportunity arose in a completely new area of business. Belfast's airport, at the time, was at Nutt's Corner. In the rudimentary buildings attached to the airport was a tearoom of sorts. There some of the workers ran a canteen which provided some minimal catering for the passengers. It was a poorly run operation and the workers' committee had great difficulty in running their modest business. Neither was there a licence for the sale of alcoholic liquor, which proved to be a real disadvantage.

By now Billy Hastings had met William Hamilton (no relation of Joy's) and they decided to form a company – Hamilton and Hastings – to run the catering at the airport. The first thing they did was to apply for a licence and, once this was approved, they set about turning the catering into a service fit for the passengers using the airport. Soon the Nutt's Corner operation was transformed into a most successful venture and a fair profit was made over the five or so years that it traded there before the airport was replaced by the new streamlined terminal at Aldergrove.

The concession to run the catering was transferred to the new airport in 1967. This time Billy realised the need for another professional to be headhunted. He offered Ben Kirk, at that time the assistant manager at the Grand Central Hotel in Belfast, the job of running this operation. Ben Kirk knew about running restaurants and he quickly turned the new facility into a profitable one. He taught Billy a great deal about the rudiments of hotel catering and

The Stormont Hotel

franchise for a further ten years before eventually selling out to Trust House Forte.

From Ireland to the Isle of Man and England

As a company Hamilton and Hastings was proving to be a very successful undertaking. It was well established at the airport and soon a further opportunity arose outside Ireland – on the Isle of Man. This was still a very popular location for holidays although, like many resorts in Ireland and elsewhere in the British Isles, it was soon to lose out to cheap package holidays to Majorca and the Spanish costas. Several openings turned up on the Isle of Man and, before long, Hamilton and Hastings, through careful diversification and investment, had bought the Peveril Hotel in Douglas for £35,000 and taken a lease on the Grand Island Hotel in Ramsey. Then, owing to their catering experience , they were granted the concession at the Sea Terminal at Douglas and at the Curraghs Wildlife Park on the island. Eventually these profitable hotels and concessions were disposed of, by which time much knowledge had been acquired.

At around the same time, the company expanded further into England where they were awarded the bar and food concessions at Teesside airport and the airport's St George's Hotel, a 60 bedroom Grade A hotel converted from a World War Two Officers' Mess. These years were profitable and greatly helped Billy in his desire finally to move out of public houses and catering concessions and achieve a further ambition – to become a hotelier. He was the first to admit his lack of expertise in the field but desperately wanted to 'dip his toe into the water' of the hotel trade.

hotel design for, although Billy was well experienced in the licensed trade, he was much less familiar with hotel management. Once again, Billy's flair in attracting the right person to the right job had worked in his favour. Hamilton and Hastings held the airport

Billy Hastings – the Hotelier

The Stormont

Life in the 1950s in Northern Ireland was relatively peaceful. Although there had been an IRA campaign between 1956 until 1962, there were still too few hotel beds to accommodate the increasing numbers of visitors to the Province. Hamilton and Hastings accordingly decided to enter the hotel business. When a large detached house called 'Dunmisk' on the Upper Newtownards Road became available, they bought it from the builder owner whose name was McMaster.

At that time it was not possible to obtain a public house licence in this part of residential east Belfast, but, if a hotel had ten or more bedrooms, then a licence could be acquired. And so the two entrepreneurs converted the house into the Stormont Hotel (so named as it was almost opposite the gates of Parliament Buildings, Stormont). They had also highlighted the archaic licensing laws in Northern Ireland and it took much campaigning to eventually persuade the Minister of Home Affairs to ease these laws. In the meantime, this hotel proved to be a highly successful establishment – and still is today.

However Billy Hastings and William Hamilton were soon to go their own separate ways. Hamilton was anxious to involve the firm in the catering franchises for Northern Ireland Railways but Billy Hastings did not want to follow this route. Sadly William Hamilton died not long after this decision and Billy bought out Hamilton's interest in the Stormont Hotel.

His ties with the business of Hamilton and Hastings were now at an end. It had been a fruitful and enterprising relationship but it was time to branch out. All other interests were sold to Ben Kirk who had helped Billy

Stormont Hotel reception area

manage the Stormont for a time. Kirk continues to trade successfully as the external caterer, Hamilton and Kirk, with his base at the King's Hall, Belfast. Billy had achieved his premier ambition. He now owned a hotel – and a fashionable and successful one - which today has 104 bedrooms, two restaurants, fine conference facilities and a four star rating.

The Adair Arms, Ballymena

In the early 1960s, Ballymena was a thriving and bustling town through which all traffic passed on its way to the north and north-west. In the centre of the town there was a fine and well frequented hotel, the Adair Arms.

The hotel came on the market in 1964 and Billy bought it for £30,000. Improvements and renovations were quickly

The Culloden Hotel

undertaken and soon the modernised Adair Arms became one of Northern Ireland's finest hotels. The high standards included 36 bedrooms, a function suite and a very popular grill bar restaurant. Once again Billy had the foresight to engage a most competent manageress, Marian Muir, who had been headhunted from the Fort Royal Hotel in Rathmullan in County Donegal. He subsequently sold this hotel as a successful business and it still prospers today.

The Culloden, Craigavad

This spectacular house, built in the Scottish baronial style and set in twelve acres of gardens, overlooks the shores of Belfast Lough at Craigavad, not far from Holywood in County Down. It had been built in 1876 by William Robinson and took over two years to complete. Most of the stone used in the construction came from Scotland by boat and, having been landed in the fairly distant little County Down port of Portaferry, the stone had then to be transported by horse and cart to Craigavad. Robinson had chosen a particularly suitable setting for his new house for the southern shore of Belfast Lough was well sheltered from the prevailing winds.

In 1964 the house was put up for sale and was auctioned by Jim Morgan of Ross's, the well-known auctioneers. There were many interested prospective purchasers in the auction room that day anxious to make bids for the property. The estimate was expected to be in the region of £13,000. Soon, however, an unknown telephone bidder made an enormous offer of £18,000. Everyone was intrigued to know the identity of the buyer and it turned out to be Rutledge White, a respected Belfast businessman. He intended to turn the Culloden into an elegant boutique hotel. The Whites were a foremost family in Belfast who already owned White's bakeries and White's milk bars.

But the purchase of the Culloden was a bigger challenge than they had anticipated. Rutledge and his wife, Madge, were determined to make the Culloden the best hotel in the country. They spent five years of devoted care to the enterprise but they could not turn it into a profitable business. However, they did accomplish a great deal. They furnished the house in a grand style which included the purchase of expensive chandeliers, wonderful French furnishings and many beautiful paintings. One of the

talking points of the Culloden was the fact that the former chapel had been turned into a bar. The house had previously been the diocesan see house for the Church of Ireland bishops of Down and Dromore. It was reputed that the Whites had the chapel deconsecrated (which is highly likely in the circumstances!) and, even to this day, there are many stories about the conversion of this area in the house into a public bar which had originally been set aside for the worship of God.

Having established the first real luxury hotel in the Province, the Whites employed one of the finest chefs of the time, who produced food which tended to be beyond the palate of the Northern Ireland public of the day. There were only 14 bedrooms and the Whites were trying to cater for

The foyer of the Culloden Hotel

The Ballygally Castle Hotel

too select a market. Madge White was so meticulous in her attention to her guests that profitability inevitably suffered. The years of hard work in the hotel business sadly came to an end for Madge and Rutledge White and they reluctantly decided to sell the hotel.

Billy Hastings was keenly interested in adding the Culloden to his hotel portfolio. In 1967, he agreed on the broad guidelines of a deal. At the crucial juncture, however, Billy was confined to bed with mumps! The finalising of the purchase was, therefore, left to his trusted accountant, Rollo McClure, who was able to inform Billy that the amount of £100,000 had been agreed with the fixtures and fittings included together with a £25,000 tax loss available, which could be claimed by his company.

Billy, from the comfort of his sick bed, approved the deal and went back to sleep!

Once again, an exceptional manager was recruited to develop the hotel. Hugh Margey was a young graduate of University College, Dublin and the son of Billy's friend, Hugh senior, who had assisted in the development of the Adair Arms Hotel in Ballymena. He was ideally qualified and delighted to accept Billy's challenge at the Culloden. Following additional investment and expansion, the Culloden became another Hastings success. Nowadays it boasts 79 bedrooms, eleven apartments, the Elysium Health Spa, the Cultra Inn and a five star rating.

The Ballygally Castle Hotel

In 1968 Cyril Lord, the carpet entrepreneur, was selling up

his interests in Northern Ireland, having decided to leave and spend his retirement in Barbados. One of his prime properties, which he had bought in the 1950s, was the beautifully situated Ballygally Castle Hotel on the world famous Antrim coast road. At the time it had 20 bedrooms and was an attractive proposition for Billy Hastings. So he bought the hotel for £40,000 and immediately set about renovating the establishment. It is now a 44 bedroom hotel with full conference facilities. This prestigious hotel remains within the Hastings Group to this day.

The castle has a long, interesting and chequered history. It was built in 1625 by a Scotsman, James Shaw, of local stone in the style of a French chateau with walls five feet thick. During the turbulent 17th century the castle was frequently attacked and plundered - yet it survived intact. The Shaw family retained ownership until the nineteenth century and, during their tenure, many additions were made to the building. The castle is reputed to be haunted by the ghost of Lady Isabelle Shaw who continues to make her presence felt by walking about the hotel passages at night attired in a silk dress and amusing herself by knocking at the bedroom doors.

The Ulster Transport Authority Hotels

Until mid 1966, Northern Ireland's major transport undertaking, the Ulster Transport Authority (UTA), had owned six large hotels in different parts of the Province. The Northern Ireland government wanted to divest itself of these facilities because they were no longer making money and were becoming a drain on the Province's finances. So they were put on the market in the hope that one of the major British or Irish chains would snap them up. In the Northern Ireland parliament at Stormont, the Minister of Development at the time, William Craig, announced that he and his parliamentary colleague, the

Minister of Commerce, Brian Faulkner, had signed a deal with Grand Metropolitan Hotels Limited whereby the six hotels were sold to them for £600,000 plus the value of food stocks, but with the important proviso that the new owners built a large new hotel in the centre of Belfast.

An agreement was made that they retained the existing staff of the hotels and they were further required to inform the government of any future intention to sell any of the hotels. The government would then be given the first offer to purchase. For the next two years or more there were regular, and often acrimonious, debates in the Northern Ireland House of Commons about this hotel deal. Many MPs, including Harry Diamond, MP for Falls, considered that the hotels had been disposed of at a giveaway price.

William Craig argued that the price of £600,000 was far greater than the £400,000 valuation of the properties. The fact, too, that the promised replacement hotel was not being built quickly enough also led to further unpleasant parliamentary exchanges. In the end, of course, the replacement – the Europa Hotel – did open its doors in mid 1971.

Maxwell Joseph of Grand Metropolitan Hotels, before finalising the deal with William Craig, insisted that the licensing laws for hotels were relaxed. Having acquiesced and introduced relevant legislation, the Minister was relieved to hear that Joseph's company was prepared to buy the hotels. Their future now seemed secure. But Joseph soon realised that the former UTA hotels did not fit in with his modern 'brand' image and it was not long before he decided to sell them and make the new Europa his flagship hotel. As far as Billy Hastings was concerned he was not even considered as a prospective buyer at that time but it was not long before he again was able not only to show his interest but also his ability to purchase these hotels.

In May 1971, the hotels were again put on the market by Maxwell Joseph. There seemed only one person willing to risk the investment required – and more importantly – the nerve to put in a bid, especially with the downturn in the economy and the growing civil unrest, and this time it was Billy Hastings. So, with the help and expertise of Rollo McClure, his accountant, and his solicitor Sir Charles Brett of Messrs L'Estrange and Brett, the hotels were bought for the sum of £440,000. Another vital cog in the wheel was Frank Hughes, Billy's co-director and right hand man.

Frank had worked closely with Billy for many years in the licensed trade and, by dint of his confidence and support, helped him create the situation whereby Hastings could make the quantum leap from public houses to major hotel ownership. Such a reliable and compatible colleague was a great strength to Billy and, between the two of them, they turned this venture to their advantage. Billy's hotel empire expanded dramatically with the purchase of these six former UTA hotels – the Northern Counties in Portrush; the Laharna in Larne; the Midland in Belfast; the City in Londonderry; the Great Northern in Rostrevor and the Slieve Donard in Newcastle. All had been excellent hotels in the past but now, for the most part, had seen better days. For Billy Hastings, however, there was some good news and some bad news to come.

The Financial Position – the Good News

At the time of his purchase of the six hotels from the UTA in 1971, Billy Hastings was established as a hotelier of influence and importance. His bars were generating revenue which helped to finance improvements to the hotels. In 1970 the business had an annual turnover of £1.6 million which was generating £100,000 in cash each year. Drinks and beverages amounted to 65% of this turnover and the remaining 35% was on food and accommodation. This showed the reliance on the funds from the public houses to help subsidise the hotel part of the business. The bottling plants had been sold and this had created much needed cash when the offer of the UTA hotels had arisen.

Throughout the troubled 1970s and beyond, the steady profits from the pubs, therefore, had been the saviour of the Group. By the mid 1970s, however, even the pubs were beginning to feel the pinch because of the proliferation of working class pubs and drinking clubs which now could apply for licences. This siphoned off both the profits and the loyal clientele from the Hastings pubs. By the end of the decade and as part of a gradual process, Billy made the decision to sell off most of the bars or lease them as property developments.

The Political Situation in Northern Ireland – the Bad News

Just at the time that Billy Hastings was buying the Culloden Hotel in 1967 and some time before he made the purchase of the former UTA hotels, the political situation in Northern Ireland was reaching fever pitch. In 1968 the Civil Rights Association had issued their demands for reforms to the then Prime Minister of Northern Ireland, Captain Terence O'Neill. By the end of the year, there was disorder on the streets and continuing political upheaval which threatened the stability of the Province. It was at exactly this inauspicious time that Billy Hastings was buying the six UTA hotels. The future looked bleak.

On 9 August 1971, the death throes of the tourist industry and the hotel trade in Northern Ireland were finally felt. Brian Faulkner, then the Prime Minister, introduced internment and the whole future for the Province was in the balance. The measure was not only ill-advised but it also sounded the death knell for the government of Northern Ireland. By the succeeding March 1972, the Westminster Conservative administration of Edward Heath had suspended the Stormont regime, leaving a Secretary of State to run the Province.

As the Troubles escalated, the tourist trade seriously declined. In the space of just two years, the number of visitors fell from over one million to just 400,000. The hotel businesses were in dire straits and Billy Hastings, as one of the Province's biggest hoteliers, had to consider his options. In order to keep the hotels open, he set about examining what he could do to reduce costs.

Requisitions for new equipment, for example, were closely examined and, where possible, an old piece of equipment remained rather than purchasing a more up-to-date model. Where an entire floor could be closed and the heating there turned off, then this was done. Belts were tightened and corners were cut where it did not involve a reduction in safety or comfort for the residents.

But there was to be a saviour for the industry. Once the ballrooms had been packed with elegant dancers gliding around the floor to the strains of a foxtrot or quickstep. Now these same ballrooms were filled with young people, this time gyrating to the strains of disco music. Soon thousands of youngsters were flocking to the Slieve Donard in Newcastle or the Northern Counties in Portrush as disco fever and roller discos hit the towns and villages of Northern Ireland.

Through necessity Billy pioneered the disco expansion in Northern Ireland and they were a godsend for it meant that on at least a couple of nights every week his hotels were making money. It did not matter that the money was not being spent on bedroom accommodation. The disco revolution had come just in time and thus were the storms of those critical years of the 1970s weathered.

In the early 1970s there also arrived a saviour for the Culloden Hotel. Like all the other hotels, the Culloden was suffering badly from an almost total lack of visitors. The 'knight in shining armour' was none other than the first Secretary of State for Northern Ireland, William Whitelaw. The newly-refurbished, yet sadly empty, 30 bedroom hotel was taken over, lock, stock and barrel, by Mr Whitelaw and his Northern Ireland Office staff. This arrangement continued when Merlyn Rees became the Secretary of State following the general election of February 1974 which brought the Labour Party to power.

For a period of over four years, there were no worries about who would be paying the Culloden bills. This left Billy with extra time and energy to turn his attention to his other locations. Hotels on the outskirts of the towns and cities, including the 40 bedroom Stormont Hotel, were doing better than those in town and city centres.

Stark Realities in a Terrorist Situation

The political and financial difficulties affecting both Northern Ireland in general and the Hastings Group in particular also brought the harsh reality of living in a disturbed society to Billy Hastings' front door. His family and friends felt the draught of cold sectarianism and brutal criminality on a number of occasions over the years.

In May 1971, when sectarian attacks were rife, a bomb was placed in one of Billy's pubs, the Mountainview Tavern on the Shankill Road in west Belfast. Many customers were critically injured and there was one death resulting from the incident. As the bodies still lay in the rubble with the

The Slieve Donard Hotel

paramedical staff endeavouring to save lives, mobs of youths were seen scrambling through the debris looting for money, drink and cigarettes. The scene revolted Billy and his friends and left an indelible mark on his mind. Not long after this shameful incident, one of his trusted employees and friends, Philip Maguire, had his van hijacked as he was delivering wage packets. His attackers, not satisfied with robbing him of the payroll, callously turned on Philip and shot him dead. The memory of this senseless and brutal murder remains with Billy to this day.

But even worse was to follow. After many threats and warnings had been issued by the terrorists that members of his family would be abducted if extortion demands were not met, Billy was himself kidnapped at gunpoint during 1978. He escaped from his Ulster Defence Association (UDA) abductors without the ransom being paid. Although no money was ever handed over and no protection demands ever paid, in spite of threats, nonetheless there were many armed robberies from his pubs and hotels. This was par for the course in those dreadful and troubled days.

Not long after buying the UTA hotels and the subsequent introduction of internment in August 1971, Billy found himself, on the very evening that the measure was enforced, seeking to enlist the support of his friends and staff to help protect his property from arson and looting. The entire terrifying night was spent at his different locations keeping howling mobs at bay. His businesses survived that night's orgy of destruction but his luck was not to hold for ever. Bomb alerts, both real and bogus, became a daily occurrence.

The grand entrance to the Slieve Donard Hotel

The Hastings Hotels Group

By the end of the 1970s the Northern Counties Hotel in Portrush and the Laharna in Larne had been sold. The Midland Hotel beside the railway station on York Road ceased functioning as a hotel and became the new Hastings Hotels Group's headquarters to replace their former HQ at the Avenue One public house on the Newtownards Road. This pub had originally been built by Billy's father. The Group took over the top floor of the former hotel and rented out the remainder of the space as offices. The Midland Building remains the Group HQ to this day.

In 1973, the City Hotel in Londonderry was disposed of as it had been bombed beyond repair. A similar fate met the once majestic Great Northern Hotel in Rostrevor when it too was burned out in a terrorist attack in 1974. This meant that the only UTA hotel still in the Group's ownership was the Slieve Donard in Newcastle. The remaining Hastings Group hotels were all extensively refurbished following huge financial investment. This consolidated the Group as the leading hotel operation in Northern Ireland.

The Slieve Donard, Newcastle

Many consider the Slieve Donard to be the jewel in the Hastings crown. This hotel has had a long and very distinguished career. It was built in 1897 at the cost of £44,000 at the peak of railway travel to the seaside. It remained the most successful venture for the Belfast and County Down Railway, which prided itself in providing a first class rail service for hotel guests. Twice every weekday and once each Saturday the railway enabled golfers to enjoy the spectacular links close to the hotel. Set amidst the magnificent surroundings of the Mourne Mountains and the beautiful Newcastle Bay, the 'Slieve' has attracted visitors from all parts of the world over the 100 years of its existence.

In those early halcyon days the Slieve Donard epitomised the finest Victorian grandeur and luxury. Its wonderfully equipped and sumptuous dining and drawing rooms, complemented by beautifully appointed bedrooms with Chippendale furniture and Persian carpets, helped to conjure up scenes of opulence and decadence. With its suites of remedial and sea baths and its douche, spray, needle and Turkish baths with water brought up from the sea by electric pumps, the hotel could rightly boast that the Slieve Donard was the ultimate place to be.

The Everglades Hotel

The rich and the famous experienced the hotel's hospitality over the past century and possibly its best known guest was Charlie Chaplin, who spent a night at the hotel in 1921. Guests were continuously entertained by the best and most accomplished artistes of the day. Famous dance bands, violinists, pianists and singers graced the hotel's portals not only in the evenings, but also by giving discreet recitals during the day as the guests ate their meals in the dining areas. The hotel became the focal point for many people with a wide range and diversity of interests.

Throughout its 100 years the hotel has been constantly upgraded and refurbished. Millions of pounds have been spent keeping the hotel in the forefront of gracious living. It has had its fair share of difficulties, especially during the years of the Troubles. It has been four times bombed but fortunately there have been very few injuries, and the repair work has always been quickly completed. The company's financial director, Edward Carson, nicknamed the hotel the 'Titanic', as he considered that it was always in peril of sinking and taking the entire company with it. It survived and remains a thriving resort hotel to this day.

During its centenary celebrations in 1997, the Slieve Donard achieved the accolade as one of the finest conference, golf and leisure hotels in the Province. VIP guests over the past ten years have included Bishop Desmond Tutu, Tiger Woods, Michael Jordan, Catherine Zeta-Jones and her husband Michael Douglas, and Judith Chalmers who described the Slieve Donard Hotel in her ITV holiday programme in 1998 as 'probably the finest hotel she had ever stayed in' – praise indeed!

Additional Purchases and Changes

In 1984 the Group bought the Fir Trees Hotel in Strabane to consolidate a presence west of the Bann following the demise of the City Hotel in Londonderry. However it could never have qualified as a four star hotel and consequently it, too, was sold following a bomb attack just prior to the purchase of the Europa Hotel. In 1993, at the same time as they were purchasing the Europa in Belfast, the Group purchased the Everglades Hotel on the outskirts of Londonderry, also from the receivers, BDO Stoy Hayward, thus showing the company's total commitment to serving the north west. By 1995 the Hastings Hotels Group was striving to ensure that all their hotels were either four star or five star facilities.

An All-Ireland Dimension

As the strongest hotel group in Northern Ireland, it seemed logical for Billy Hastings and his board to attempt to gain a foothold in the Republic of Ireland to expand their operation into an all-Ireland one. The chance to invest in the south came in 1995 when Billy announced a joint venture with two leading wealthy entrepreneurs based in Dublin, Lochlann Quinn and Martin Naughton of the Glen Electric Group.

Plans were implemented to spend well over £20 million on the new five star Merrion Hotel in the Irish capital's fashionable Merrion Street. When the 145 bedroom hotel opened at Easter 1997, it was the most expensive hotel project in Ireland. It had been fashioned out of a terrace of four exquisite Georgian houses directly opposite the Irish Parliament building, the Dail. One of the houses, Mornington House, was reputed to have been the birthplace of the Duke of Wellington and, at the time of the Boer War, the entire terrace had been a sanatorium for

Merrion Hotel, Dublin

convalescing soldiers returning from South Africa.

In its latter days, because of its proximity to the Dail, the houses had served as government offices. The enterprise has been an outstanding success. As holder of a 50% share in this prestigious Georgian property, Billy Hastings has firmly stamped his not inconsiderable influence on this first ever all-Ireland hotel company.

The Chairman's Contributions to Local Society

Apart from his business interests, Billy Hastings has always been a great believer in making a contribution to society. With his social conscience, he has held various positions which have brought him into close contact with many people in all walks of life. The sociability of his membership of outside organisations has given Billy a great deal of satisfaction and pleasure. From his early days in the Vintners' Association, Billy has variously been chairman of the Hotel and Catering Association,

Joy and Billy

president of the Chamber of Commerce, chairman of the Institute of Directors, a member of the Northern Ireland Tourist Board, president of the Northern Ireland Institute of Marketing, a board member of Bass Ireland for twenty five years and a Lloyd's underwriter.

On the charity side, he has been chairman of Help the Aged (Northern Ireland), chairman of the Prince's Trust Volunteers, president of the Chest, Heart and Stroke Association (Northern Ireland) and is a patron of Polio Plus. He is a regular worshipper and a board member at Down Cathedral, the burial place of Ireland's three best known and most celebrated saints, Patrick, Brigid and Columba.

One of the bravest public duty steps Billy Hastings has ever taken was his election to Belfast City Council for the Pottinger ward, where many of his pubs were located, during the darkest days for the Province. In 1970, the end of Stormont looked more and more likely with the probability of direct rule from London. Many politicians wanted Billy to get more involved in politics but he was not interested and, after just three years, he did not seek re-election.

Now well into his seventies, Billy Hastings continues to enjoy getting up every morning and heading for work. More and more, of course, his children run the business but they are always shrewd enough to seek their father's – or the Chairman's – advice. He believes in a work discipline and in paying accounts promptly. He would admit that this might be considered a little old fashioned but his father instilled this trait into him, and this, in turn, he has instilled into his own children. He never has had any intention of floating the company on the stock market. He believes that if the money you are spending is your own, then you work harder to improve your own company. It is the philosophy he has taught his family.

Billy is an optimist. He likes to face up to any problem immediately before troubles multiply. He has had ups and downs and some disappointments but overall he feels that, with his inbuilt enthusiasm, he can bring out the best in the people he meets and influences. He was honoured in 1986 by the University of Ulster with an Honorary Doctorate in recognition of his support to the university's hotel and catering departments and was the recipient of an OBE for his services to the tourism industry in 1985.

In the Queen's Birthday Honours list of June 2003, his OBE was advanced to CBE for his continued contributions to tourism and the economy. He hopes for a better future for the Province – a place which he will ever greatly love.

The greatest asset to the organisation is, undoubtedly, the chairman, Billy Hastings himself. He has been described variously throughout the years in one interview after another as avuncular, genial and relaxed. His energy and dynamism are legendary. He has the enthusiasm of a man who regularly puts to shame the efforts of people half his age. Having successfully overcome the rigours of his early years in the bar trade in Belfast in the 1960s, Billy Hastings fully intends to continue to show his perseverance and indomitable spirit, in pursuit of hotel excellence in Northern Ireland – Hastings Hotels style.

The Europa in the Twenty First Century

Life in the hotel and catering industry has changed beyond all recognition since those elegant bygone days of steam travel and exclusive seaside hotels when railway owners set the pace for travellers and holiday makers. Gone are the resident orchestras and fashionable ballrooms of a century ago.

Nowadays conference packages, wedding extravaganzas, spa leisure developments and golf courses have readily been provided by hotel managements in response to their guests' ever changing demands. New ideas, eye-pleasing architecture, better food and ever improved services have evolved in the on-going search to attract more and more business from every corner of the world. The Belfast Europa has become every bit as important to the Northern Ireland's economy as is the Mirage in Las Vegas to the United States and the Burj al Arab in Dubai to the United Arab Emirates.

Europa Hotel staff, September 2003
A World Class Hotel – Past and Present

Thus, in the early 1970s, Billy Hastings watched as the new Europa Hotel appeared on the urban landscape. He was well aware of William Craig's and the Northern Ireland government's dilemma with the Province's hotel industry and its struggling UTA hotels. He had then seen Maxwell Joseph of Grand Metropolitan commit his company to providing Belfast with a world-class hotel. Unfortunately for both Maxwell Joseph and for the law-abiding citizens of Northern Ireland, however, the Troubles soon severely compromised his commitment and the government's strategic plan for the city. His brilliant ideas for an ultra modern hotel did not have the chance to achieve their full potential.

The 1970s was a decade which stunted growth and dampened enthusiasm, and, with a heavy heart, Maxwell Joseph finally left Belfast disillusioned. But when the Europa was eventually purchased by Billy Hastings in 1993, it was he who took the opportunity to bring to fruition the hopes and aspirations that Maxwell Joseph had envisioned twenty years earlier.

Opportunities for the Next Hastings Generation

The Hastings Hotels Group is essentially a family business. What profits they make are immediately ploughed back into the hotels to ensure a first class service to all their customers. Being a private company, it is not constrained by demands from external shareholders and can

Onwards and Upwards

Life in the hotel and catering industry has changed beyond all recognition since those elegant ... of steam travel and

response to their guests' ever changing demands. New ideas, eye-pleasing architecture, better food and ever improved services have evolved in the on-going ...

Thus, in the early 1970s, Billy Hastings watched as the new Europa Hotel appeared on the urban landscape. He was well aware of William Craig's and the Northern Ireland government's dilemma with the Province's

Chapter 8

The Europa in the Twenty-First Century

Visions and Ambitions

Life in the hotel and catering industry has changed beyond all recognition since those elegant bygone days of steam travel and exclusive seaside hotels when railway owners set the pace for travellers and holiday makers. Gone are the resident orchestras and fashionable ballrooms of a century ago.

Nowadays conference packages, wedding extravaganzas, spa leisure developments and golf courses have readily been provided by hotel managements in response to their guests' ever changing demands. New ideas, eye-pleasing architecture, better food and ever improved services have evolved in the on-going search to attract more and more business from every corner of the world. The Belfast Europa has become every bit as important to the Northern Ireland economy as is the Mirage in Las Vegas to the United States, and the Burj al Arab in Dubai to the United Arab Emirates.

A World Class Hotel – Past and Present

In the early 1970s, Billy Hastings watched as the new Europa Hotel appeared on the urban landscape. He was well aware of William Craig's and the Northern Ireland government's dilemma with the Province's hotel industry and its struggling UTA hotels. He had then seen Maxwell

Joseph of Grand Metropolitan commit his company to providing Belfast with a world-class hotel. Unfortunately for both Maxwell Joseph and for the law-abiding citizens of Northern Ireland, the Troubles soon severely compromised his commitment and the government's strategic plan for the city. His brilliant ideas for an ultra modern hotel did not have the chance to achieve their full potential.

The 1970s was a decade which stunted growth and dampened enthusiasm, and, with a heavy heart, a disillusioned Maxwell Joseph finally left Belfast . But when the Europa was eventually purchased by Billy Hastings in 1993, it was he who took the opportunity to bring to fruition the hopes and aspirations that Maxwell Joseph had envisioned twenty years earlier.

Opportunities for the Next Hastings Generation

The Hastings Hotels Group is essentially a family business. What profits they make are immediately ploughed back into the hotels to ensure a first class service to all their customers. Being a private company, it is not constrained by demands from external shareholders and can invest for the long-term. The Group realises that it needs to listen to customers, continually improve relationships with suppliers and, above all, keep abreast of all the most up to date marketing techniques. Unlike large hotel chains, there is nowhere to pass the buck; to rest on their laurels is not an option for the family.

Billy also realised the need to consider his company's future and whether or not the next generation of the Hastings family would be prepared to become part of the business. As the opportunities arose, he invited his four children - Julie, Howard, Allyson and Aileen - to participate in the company, if this was their desire. Not wanting to unduly influence or force them into any premature decisions, and wanting them to be able to hold their own, he advised them to gain experience in other businesses. By the time they all did decide to join their father's company, they had already been successful in their own respective careers, representing an eclectic mix of skills, which will ensure the future of the Europa in particular and for Hastings Hotels in general.

Julie Maguire, the eldest daughter and marketing director, joined the firm in 1988 with a degree from Queen's University, Belfast, a Master's degree from the University of Georgia in the United States and a Post Graduate diploma in Marketing from the University of Ulster. Her experience in market research, the travel business and the world of computers admirably equipped Julie for her developing career within the organisation.

She has developed e-marketing strategies using on-line databases and has been successful in selling directly on the internet. Working closely with local and national press, advertising agencies, design companies and public relations initiatives, Julie has heightened the Hastings 'brand' image in the marketplace and kept it well ahead of its competitors.

Networking is the most important aspect of sales. As sales director, Aileen Martin, the youngest daughter, makes it her business to know all the sales representatives and ensures that the Hastings name is kept to the forefront. Aileen has a degree from Stirling University and a post graduate diploma in marketing from the University of Ulster. She spent valuable time working in Scotland selling wines and spirits to hotels and pubs. This experience has proved beneficial in her role within the company and she plans sales campaigns with Julie's expert help in preparing back-up marketing material, brochures and exhibition stands in order to sell more effectively.

Allyson Hastings, the middle daughter, is events director. Having worked in London and in Spain for ten years, together with considerable public relations skills, and with a Higher National Diploma and a degree from Buckingham College and a BA (Hons) degree from the

The Hastings Hotel directors. Top (l-r): John Toner, Julie Maguire, Aileen Martin. Bottom (l-r): Howard Hastings, Dr Billy Hastings, Joy Hastings, Allyson Hastings, Edward Carson

Dr Billy Hastings with Julie, Howard, Aileen and Allyson outside Culloden Hotel

changes and improvements are needed to ensure the company's leading place in Northern Ireland. Howard has been chairman of the local Institute of Directors and has served on the boards of Investors in People (UK) and the Bank of Ireland. His reputation amongst the business community in Northern Ireland continues to grow as he now participates on the board of Tourism Ireland, a north/south marketing body which was established as a result of the Good Friday Agreement.

Billy has had two particularly close and valued colleagues with him in the business throughout the years; the late Frank Hughes, a skilled and dependable associate, and Edward Carson, who has been with the organisation since 1972 and is now finance director and vice chairman. He has been part of the company's success story and his sound advice and expert judgement, especially at the time of the purchase of the Europa Hotel in 1993, have proved invaluable. He raised the status of the Europa as it became the most profitable of the Hastings hotels and sees the company further expanding into the Republic of Ireland, beyond the Merrion Hotel investment. A quiet and assured man, Edward is held in high regard by all those within the organisation and is highly respected in the world of business and commerce in Belfast.

John Toner's appointment in 1998, after a number of years of excellent service, as a company director with special responsibility for managing the Europa, also strengthened the skill mix within the Group. In September 2003, he moved to the Slieve Donard Hotel in his home town of Newcastle, County Down, in advance of a £10 million expansion to the resort and spa hotel. He has returned to a much changed hotel where, in 1971, he was its youngest manager at the age of 23.

James McGinn, who was appointed general manager in September 2003, is the youngest ever general manager at

University of Ulster, she is the director who works face to face with the customers organising conferences, weddings and a variety of important events.

Howard, Billy and Joy's only son, has been managing director of the Group since 1995. He holds a Law degree and is a qualified Chartered Accountant and, before joining the Group in 1989, he spent six years working and gaining valuable experience in England. He has a clear vision for the future and sees his most important job to guide the Group forward and continually to consider what

The Hastings family

and most difficult times during the 1970s and 1980s. His conviction and dedication were exemplified when, as he inspected damage caused by a bomb at the Slieve Donard Hotel in the 1980s, he turned to John Toner, who was then the general manager, and said that now, at last, he could make vital changes in the reception area! This ability to turn adversity into advantage epitomised the optimistic attitude of this hotelier extraordinaire.

The situation in Northern Ireland could hardly have been worse during those early years. Life had seemed relatively peaceful in the Province in the late 1960s with the government of Northern Ireland sharing in the buoyant mood felt throughout the United Kingdom. The introduction of internment and the emergent Troubles, culminating in the fall of the Province's administration in 1972, heralded the total disintegration of any sort of normality.

the Europa. Holding degrees from both Queen's University and the University of Ulster, James is well qualified to take the Europa forward over the coming years. He came to Hastings Hotels as quality manager in the Europa in 1996 before being promoted as general manager at the Stormont Hotel in 1999. He then gained further promotion when he went to the 5 star Culloden Hotel as general manager. The vision once held by Harper Brown 30 years ago to put the Europa on a par with the top hotels in London, New York and other major cities in the world is now the key focus for James.

The Hastings story is one of success, of hard work and determination. The family ethos is to expect everyone in the company to work hard but never as hard as the family members themselves. Above all it is a story of faith and vision. This commitment was remarkable at a time when Northern Ireland was collapsing under the deadly strains of terrorist assault. Billy built up his hotels in the hardest

With the marked downturn in the economy during the 1970s and the start of the hunger strikes in 1981, came the total collapse of the tourist market. The first glimmer of hope eventually appeared by the mid 1980s during the time when Emerald Hotels owned the Europa and peace talks were finally convened. President Clinton's visit in 1995 provided a welcome boost to the fortunes of hotels and catering establishments when visitors from all parts of the world once again arrived in Northern Ireland in greater numbers than had been seen for years.

By the time of the signing of the Belfast Agreement in 1998, life had almost returned to normal until the Omagh bomb dealt a further blow. Nobody could ever have known at the time that the ceasefires were going to be announced in 1994 soon after the purchase of the Europa, but Billy's determination paid off and the new look Europa has been a remarkable success.

Ongoing Investment and Modernisation

Life in Northern Ireland has changed radically in the past decade. With peace now a reality, the numbers of tourists and conference delegates has increased many fold. However the terrorist attacks on New York and Washington on 11 September 2001 and the subsequent Gulf War in Iraq has, understandably, adversely affected the number of visitors from the United States and further afield and it will take time for confidence in travel to be restored.

However business travel, on which the Europa depends, has now almost fully recovered and, with the United Nations' announcement that Northern Ireland is now the second safest place in the world to visit (after Japan), the Group is looking forward to the day when visitor numbers will equal those in the rest of the United Kingdom.

James McGinn, general manager of the Europa from September 2003

The 'peace dividend' has brought with it many responsibilities for everyone and none more so than for those in the hotel industry. Vacancies in the hotel trade now

provide significant employment opportunities. The arrival of the big hotel 'brand' names – Hilton, Holiday Inn, Ramada, Days, Jury's and Radisson, to name but a few – has helped to sharpen the wits of all involved in the industry, and significantly altered the markets in which Hastings Hotels operate. Competition helps to raise standards.

Today's visitors to the Europa can scarcely appreciate the many changes which have taken place since the Europa was built in 1971. The Hastings philosophy of continuous investment to ensure that their guests' needs are delivered has seen the fabric of all aspects of hotel life continually updated in line with the latest housekeeping trends.

Thirty years ago, for example, reservations were made by telephone or telex. The telex then gave way to the fax machine which, in turn, led to further growth in Information Technology. Computer systems now manage reservations and the advent of electronic mail as an instant means of communication has accelerated these changes. In 2003 the Hastings Hotels website, www.hastingshotels.com was named the BT Northern Ireland/*Belfast Telegraph* e-Xcellence award winner of the year. The judges commended the site's e-Commerce capabilities, its secure online booking facility and the wealth of information available to its potential customers.

Europa staff needed to maintain contact with secretaries and personal assistants who made the bookings. Nowadays many hotel bookings are made by agents and not by the individual customer. Companies now contract specialists to make their staff's travel and hotel arrangements. Internet bookings and deals struck with loyalty card companies are popular with individual visitors. For hotel owners life became very complicated with so many different commissions being charged on room rates for their corporate customers. Small wonder that hotels were keen to offer special rates to guests who simply made their reservation and paid directly!

Innovation and Image Management

Innovation is essential to the hotel business. Improved technology in ovens has, for instance, made possible the introduction of the 'platinum service' (as opposed to the former 'silver service') at large banquets, which has ensured a consistency of quality and presentation of meals for every guest, as well as an enhanced speed of service. This means that the atmosphere in the kitchens is now much calmer and

Billy Hastings and Paddy McAnerney swap jobs for a day

less frantic. Gone are the days when waiting staff needed to come to table on five separate occasions to lay the heated plate, serve the joint, bring the vegetables, serve up the potatoes and finally arrive with the sauce. Chefs and waiting staff alike can now focus on improved presentation and the finer points of attending to their guests at table.

A Marketing Strategy

The future for a healthy business is bound up in sharp and focused marketing. New customers need to be attracted and existing ones carefully nurtured. All staff within the organisation are encouraged to make suggestions for improving their market share and for different ways of making life even more comfortable and appealing for their customers. There are visions of making the hotels in the Group even more golf friendly, by aspiring to make their facilities as good as those at such a major venue as Gleneagles; more health conscious, by introducing the best spa amenities available, and more conference orientated, by providing the state-of-the-art purpose-built Eurobusiness Centre at the Europa.

Visitors, especially those from overseas, are more and more critical and expect services that are second to none. Hastings Hotels are geared to provide ever better quality, as in the new executive suites in the Europa, as well as its splendid new Elephant Room night club.

Marketing strategy is probably the most important weapon in the Hastings armoury. They appreciate the continuing need to consolidate and improve relations with the public sector, with organisations such as Tourism Ireland, the Northern Ireland Tourist Board and the Belfast Visitor and Convention Bureau and with representatives of national airlines and the prospective customers themselves.

The Europa Staff - the Key to Continued Success

The Europa has always been totally reliant on the quality of its staff. They are the hotel's 'internal customers', and are the key to the success of Hastings Hotels. When the Europa was built in the early 1970s, a reliable staff team was essential and the norm. When the Hastings Group purchased the Europa in 1993, it would have been possible to introduce the 'budget' service model of the 'no frills' hotels of the 1980s and 1990s. The directors firmly rejected this approach as they were determined to offer all the services expected of a prestigious city centre hotel.

In recent times the directors have brought in various schemes to give their staff every opportunity to achieve their highest possible potential within the company. Investment in staff training has already yielded benefits. Rates of pay are as good as any in the trade and personal achievements are remunerated accordingly. Schemes have been introduced whereby prospective new members of staff are given time to spend on placement in all of the hotels throughout the Group.

Many full-time staff have been with the Europa through the Emerald and the Hastings ownership including Carolyn Stalker at reception, Mary Teeney on reservations, the executive chef, Gerry Rosato, the head concierge, Martin Mulholland, and the maintenance manager, Alan Turnbull. A number of Europa staff like bar managers Paddy McAnerney and Alan Williamson, accounts administrator, Oonagh Johnston and Rose Nagra, human resources manager, have also worked in other Hastings hotels over the years and Philip Drennan and Jennifer McLornan, both now based at the Culloden, spent many years at the Europa.

Above all, statistics show that Hastings Hotel staff remain longer in their jobs with the company than is the case with other hotels. The Hastings Group has capitalised on the importance of the many benefits in recruitment, training and on-going investment in good staff relations. The Europa has been shaped by the people who work there and the loyalty of its key members of staff be they full-time, part-time or casual, has been exemplary.

The Crown magazine is the Hastings Hotels quarterly newsletter

Carrying the Baton Forward

Billy Hastings has established himself as both the premier hotelier in Northern Ireland and one of its most successful local entrepreneurs. The Hastings Group has retained a distinctive family approach that the bigger brands will never be able to emulate. This is their trump card, an advantage which should be protected. The people of Northern Ireland can identify with the family. Many

The new September 2003 general manager appointments: Richard Robinson, Culloden; John Toner, Slieve Donard, James McGinn, Europa

recognise their Battle of Hastings '1066' car registrations and latterly the '1066' suffixes on all their hotel telephone and mobile phone numbers.

The price of such loyalty and respect is responsibility, and the necessity always to keep one step ahead of the opposition. This is a tough lesson to learn especially when a fickle public can so easily change its mind. Whereas big companies can hide behind the mask of anonymity, there is no such luxury for the Hastings family business. The Group will remain in the critical public eye, working to improve services continually – to refurbish, to renovate, and to reinvest – and it will continue to be the socially conscious organisation which the chairman has always led.

This testimonial from the Rt. Hon. Peter Brooke, MP, who was Secretary of State from 1989 until 1992, sums up exactly what Billy Hastings has meant, not only to his own organisation, but also to the hotel trade throughout Northern Ireland. 'Mine has been a walking on part in Northern Ireland affairs over the past three years. Dr Hastings' part, over the past twenty five years, has been to expand from the base of a Grade C hotel in County Antrim to controlling more than 50% of the Grade A hotel accommodation in the Province. That, against the background of Northern Ireland's Troubles, is a remarkable example of leadership, in constancy, in prescience and in stamina, and in a field which represents the broad highway back to normality'.

The Europa Hotel has now been a showpiece in the Hastings Hotels Group portfolio since 1993. Taking over the Europa at that time was a leap of faith, which is now beginning to pay dividends. The hotel, with its splendid new suites and first class décor, has proved to be a real success with thousands of satisfied customers enjoying its facilities and passing on their enthusiasm to friends and acquaintances.

Prestigious Events

The Europa, once known as 'the most bombed hotel in the world', has been transformed by commitment and hard work to be recognised as one of the friendliest hotels.

Its aims and ambitions are infinite. It has been proud to have been involved in so many prestigious events in Northern Ireland over the past decade from the Tall Ships visit in 1993 to the Clinton visits in 1995 and 1998; from the World Irish Dancing Championships in 2001 to the 2002 World Amateur Boxing Championships and the Special Olympics which took place in towns and cities throughout Ireland in 2003.

The 'Brand' of the Future

The new Hastings generation has already established a new trend in the hotel industry. The first ten years of ownership of the prestigious Europa Hotel have clearly demonstrated their vision for the way forward. The Hastings 'brand' is acknowledged as the high-flying top-notch name for luxury and excellence for its valued customers. It stands head and shoulders above the opposition which surrounds it. Having now consolidated its presence on the island of Ireland, the objective for Hastings Hotels is to expand even further afield.

The motivation of the next generation is, therefore, to push beyond the bounds of Northern Ireland and to establish the Hastings name throughout the world.

The twenty-first century, with its modern and sophisticated computerised hotel systems, has placed the Europa right in the forefront in providing accommodation second-to-none. The new generation is poised to attain new heights.

That Vision for the Future

The hope and expectation for the Europa in the twenty first century is for it to become a world famous 'trophy' hotel with its name standing as an equal alongside Gleneagles, the Mandarin Oriental and Sandy Lane. The Belfast Europa's reputation for attracting global conferences and attracting visitors from all over the world will travel before it far and wide. Its local standing for good quality food and service will be second-to-none. Its well qualified and highly motivated staff will go from strength to strength.

Good relations with the public sector and national airlines will ensure that the government is lobbied to encourage more direct flights to Belfast from Europe and North America, which will greatly benefit the tourism industry and the economy of Northern Ireland.

The continued input of staff into the future of the Europa will be encouraged by the family directors, who appreciate the total involvement by everyone concerned. The high standards set by Maxwell Joseph and Harper Brown in the heady days of the Europa in the 1970s and 1980s, despite all the great difficulties of the time, will be consolidated and surpassed. In the present times of peace and renewed prosperity, the Europa will continue

Gerry Rosato, executive chef at the Europa

139

to take the lead in Belfast's return to normality.

In an era of global 'brands', and cityscapes rendered anonymous by generic retail facades, it is remarkable that a hotel with worldwide acclaim and recognition like the Europa should be owned and managed by a local company such as Hastings Hotels. Belfast, however, is no ordinary city, and the Europa is an icon of which its citizens remain justifiably proud.

Acknowledgements

I wish to express my thanks to Dr Billy Hastings, his daughter, Julie Maguire, and the other members of the Hastings family, Howard, Allyson, Aileen and Joy, for commissioning me to write this truly fascinating and interesting story of the colossus which is the Belfast Europa Hotel. I have received nothing but kindness and helpfulness as I endeavoured to come to grips with this most unique of chronicles. Julie was the inspiration behind the project and, above all, a tireless worker in finding so much information for the book.

There are many other people I'd wish to thank too.

To my partner, Thomas Johnston, who spent many hours preparing layout and designs;

To Michael Maguire, Sam Butler, Earl Colwell and the others who assisted with editing the manuscript;

To so many past and present staff members who contributed and assisted, especially John Toner, John O'Carroll, Michael Williamson, Mima Harper, Sally Brown, Paddy McAnerney, Martin Mulholland, Mary Teeney, Jennifer McLornan, Philip Drennan, Gareth Jones, Jimmy Connor, Peter Burke, Rae McParland and former Penthouse Poppet, Evelyn Sullivan;

To the many journalists who had, in their early careers, been posted as correspondents to the Europa – Simon Hoggart, John Sergeant, Bob Chesshyre, Chris Ryder, Derek Brown, James Leavey, Deric Henderson, Sir Max Hastings, Conor O'Clery and Renagh Holohan;

To those who supplied photographs – Stephen Davidson, John Harrison, Chris Hill, Carolyn Stalker, the National Library of Ireland and the Ulster Folk and Transport Museum;

To Joyce and Norman Topley and John Miskimmin for their help with historical information about the railways;

To Stephen Prenter of BDO Stoy Hayward;

To Thomson Brown, Harper Brown's brother;

To Trevor McClintock, the former managing director of Gilbey's;

To the members of the local and national media - the BBC, UTV, *Belfast Telegraph, News Letter, Irish News, Sunday Life* and *Sunday World,* for their support and interest.

I especially want to thank Senator George Mitchell and General John de Chastelain for their messages of support and former President Bill Clinton for his words of hope and encouragement to the staff of the Europa.

Above all I wish to express my thanks to all the present day staff at the Europa for their interest. I trust that they will enjoy reading the book.

In thanking named people as I have done, I am conscious of perhaps forgetting someone in my endeavour to list everyone who helped. If I have omitted anyone's name who did give me help and advice, I would ask to be forgiven and to say thanks to them as well.

Clive Scoular
Killyleagh
County Down
October 2003